YO-BPT-317

patterns grammar

graphs charts

FLASH FORWARD

TEST PREP

spelling context

Written by **Christy Yaros**

Illustrations by **Chris Murphy**

Cover illustration by Hector Borlasca
Cover design by Loira Walsh
Interior design by Gladys Lai
Edited by Eliza Berkowitz

Flash Kids
A Division of Barnes & Noble
122 Fifth Ave
New York, NY 10011

ISBN: 978-1-4114-1619-2

Please submit all inquiries to FlashKids@bn.com

Printed and bound in the United States

1 3 5 7 9 10 8 6 4 2

Dear Parent,

Test taking can be challenging for kids. In the face of test questions, answer bubbles, and the ticking clock, it's easy to see why tests can be overwhelming. That's why it's vital that children prepare for tests beforehand. Knowing the material is only part of preparing for tests. It's equally important that children practice answering different types of questions, filling in answers, and pacing themselves through test material. Children who practice taking tests develop confidence and can relax during the real test.

This Flash Forward Test Prep book will give your child the opportunity to practice taking tests in reading and math. Each practice test is based on national standards, so you know your child is reviewing important material he or she should be learning in the fifth grade. In addition to reinforcing fifth-grade curriculum, this book allows your child to practice answering different kinds of test questions. Best of all, each unit ends with a four-page practice test that reviews all the material in that unit. This truly gives kids a chance to show what they know and to see their progress.

The more practice children have before taking a test, the more relaxed and confident they will be during the exam. As your child works through the book, he or she will start to develop test-taking strategies. These strategies can be utilized during a real test. By the time your child finishes the book, he or she will be ready to tackle any exam, from the annual standardized test to the weekly pop quiz!

Table of Contents

Test-Taking Tips

Preparing for a test starts with your mind and body. Here are some things you can do before the test to make sure you're ready.

- A few days before the test, get together with friends from your class to review the material. Have fun quizzing each other.

- The night before the test, go to bed early and get plenty of sleep.

- Eat a healthy breakfast the morning of the test.

- Find out beforehand if you need a pencil, eraser, or pen, and make sure you pack them in your schoolbag.

- Before you leave for school, do a few practice test questions at home to get warmed up.

- Remember to use the restroom before the test begins.

- Have confidence in yourself. A positive attitude will help you do well!

Once the test has started, you need to stay focused. Here are some tips to keep in mind during the test.

- Always begin by reading or listening carefully to the directions.

- Make sure you read all the answer choices before choosing the one you think is correct.

- If you get stuck on a certain question, it's okay to skip it. Go back to the question later.

- Work at your own pace. Don't pay attention to how quickly other students are completing the test.

- Fill in the answer bubbles completely and neatly.

- If you finish the test before time is up, use the time to review your answers.

- Take time to double check any questions you felt uncertain about. Make sure you want to stick with your answer.

Here are some tips to keep in mind when taking reading and language tests.

- Read each question or passage slowly and carefully.

- Say words in your head and think about the sounds.

- Underline important words in the question that tell you what you need to do.

- As you read a passage, underline key words and phrases.

- Use context clues to help figure out the meaning of a word you might not know.

- Cross out answers you know are wrong. Then focus on the remaining choices.

- It's okay to go back to the passage or sentence and reread it.

These tips will help you as you work on math tests.

- Find out if you can use a piece of scratch paper or part of the test booklet to work through math problems.

- Make sure you understand each question before you choose an answer. Reread the question if you need to.

- Solve a problem twice and make sure you get the same answer both times.

- Try plugging in the answer choices to see which one makes a true math sentence.

- When you're solving word problems or story problems, underline key words that tell you what to do.

- Draw a picture to help you visualize the right answer.

- Pay attention to the operation signs and make sure you know if you need to add, subtract, multiply, or divide.

Section 1: Reading
Finding Facts

Read the passage and answer the questions.

Inventions That Save Lives

Inventors are curious about how the world works. They come up with ways to fix problems. Some inventions make our lives safer. Some inventions change the way we live.

In 1966, an American chemist named Stephanie Kwolek invented Kevlar, a type of plastic that is stronger than steel but does not weigh very much. Her invention was used to make bulletproof vests. These Kevlar vests are light to wear but strong enough to protect a person from a gunshot. Many police officers' lives have been saved by Kwolek's Kevlar vests.

Gasoline fires cannot be extinguished with water. In the 1940s, Percy Lavon Julian came up with a foam spray that stopped gas flames fast. The foam covered the fire and kept air from getting to it, so it wasn't able to burn. Today the foam spray is used in many home fire extinguishers.

Elevators make getting to the top of tall buildings fast and easy. Many years ago, the first elevators used ropes that sometimes broke, causing the elevator to crash. In 1853, Elisha Otis invented a safety elevator with arms that grabbed the sides of the elevator shaft if the ropes broke. People felt safer riding in elevators with Otis's invention. Soon, very tall buildings were built without fear of elevator accidents.

Driving at night on a dark road is dangerous. In 1934, Percy Shaw created "cat's eyes," which are little reflectors that are set in the road. A flexible rubber "eyelid" wipes the reflector clean when a car runs over it. It helps drivers to see at night.

These are just a few important inventions. These inventors saw something that needed improving, and each used his or her imagination and cleverness to create products that have made our lives better.

1. Which of these inventions came first?
   A safety elevators
   B cat's eyes
   C fire extinguishers
   D Kevlar vests

2. What is the eyelid made out of on a cat's eye?
   A plastic
   B steel
   C foam
   D rubber

3. What year was the cat's eye invented?
   A 1834
   B 1934
   C 1940
   D 1966

4. Who invented Kevlar vests?
   A Elisha Otis
   B Percy Shaw
   C Stephanie Kwolek
   D Percy Kevlar

5. How did Percy Lavon Julian's spray stop gas fires?
   A It had water in it.
   B It gave the fire air.
   C It had rubber in it to pound out the flames.
   D It covered the flames and kept the air away.

6. What material is Kevlar made from?
   A foam
   B steel
   C rubber
   D plastic

7. Which invention featured arms?
   A Kevlar
   B fire extinguishers
   C safety elevators
   D cat's eyes

8. Who invented cat's eyes?
   A Percy Lavon Julian
   B Percy Shaw
   C Stephanie Kwolek
   D Elisha Otis

9. Which invention was the most recent?
   A Kevlar vests
   B cat's eyes
   C fire extinguishers
   D safety elevators

10. What is an important feature of the Kevlar vest?
    A It is made of rubber.
    B It is light to wear.
    C It has safety arms.
    D It is made of steel.

Sequencing

Read the story and answer the questions.

Giving Thanks

Holidays were always a big deal in Caitlyn's family, but this year Thanksgiving was more special than ever before. Her brother, Steve, was home from college.

Caitlyn had a lot to do to make this Thanksgiving special. First, four days before Thanksgiving, Caitlyn painted a big banner that said "Welcome home Steve!" and set it out to dry.

The next day, Caitlyn ran errands with her mother. First, they went to the supermarket. Then they stopped by the post office to mail a letter. Finally, Caitlyn and her mother went to the party store to get decorations.

Two days before Thanksgiving, Caitlyn and her mother decorated the house. First, they made paper turkey place cards for the table. Next, they hung up the banner. Last, they put the Thanksgiving tablecloth and place mats on the dining room table.

The day before Thanksgiving, Caitlyn and her father picked up Grandma from the airport, and then stopped at Lewin's Farm to get the turkey. Later that night, Caitlyn and Grandma baked the apple and sweet potato pies, made the appetizers, and cut up the vegetables.

When Steve walked in the door Thanksgiving morning, the first thing Caitlyn did was give him a huge hug. Then she showed him the banner she made. Steve's smile let her know that this *was* going to be the best Thanksgiving ever. They had so much to give thanks for this year.

1. When did Caitlyn go to the supermarket?
   (A) four days before Thanksgiving
   (B) three days before Thanksgiving
   (C) two days before Thanksgiving
   (D) the day before Thanksgiving

2. What was the first thing Caitlyn did to prepare for Thanksgiving?
   (A) bake the pies
   (B) go to the supermarket
   (C) make the banner
   (D) go to the party store

3. Where did Caitlyn go right before she went to Lewin's Farm?
   (A) the supermarket
   (B) the party store
   (C) her grandmother's house
   (D) the airport

4. Which of these did Caitlyn do the day before Thanksgiving?
   (A) hang up the banner
   (B) bake the pies
   (C) hug Steve
   (D) make place cards

5. What was the first thing Caitlyn did when Steve walked in the door?
   (A) She gave him a hug.
   (B) She showed him the banner.
   (C) She told him about school.
   (D) She waved hello to him.

6. When did Caitlyn go to the post office?
   (A) after the party store
   (B) after the airport
   (C) after Lewin's Farm
   (D) after the supermarket

7. When did the house get decorated?
   (A) the day before Thanksgiving
   (B) two days before Thanksgiving
   (C) three days before Thanksgiving
   (D) four days before Thanksgiving

8. What is the last thing Caitlyn did to get ready for Thanksgiving?
   (A) cut up the vegetables
   (B) hang up the banner
   (C) make the turkey
   (D) put on the tablecloth

9. When did Caitlyn hang up the banner?
   (A) in between baking the pies and cutting the vegetables
   (B) in between going to the airport and Lewin's Farm
   (C) in between making the place cards and putting on the tablecloth
   (D) in between going to the supermarket and the party store

10. What did Caitlyn do right after she made the banner?
    (A) She hung it up.
    (B) She set it out to dry.
    (C) She showed it to Steve.
    (D) She showed it to her mother.

Character, Setting, and Plot

Read the story and answer the questions.

"Drink Me"

from *Alice in Wonderland* by Lewis Carroll

Alice opened the door and found that it led into a small passage, not much larger than a rat-hole. She knelt down and looked into the loveliest garden. How she longed to get out of that dark hall, but she could not even get her head though the doorway. "And even if my head would go through," thought poor Alice, "it would be of very little use without my shoulders. Oh, how I wish I could shut up like a telescope! I think I could, if I only knew how to begin." For, you see, so many out-of-the-way things had happened lately, that Alice had begun to think that very few things indeed were really impossible.

So she went back to the table: This time she found a little bottle on it, with the words "DRINK ME" on it. Alice was not going to do *that* in a hurry. "No, I'll look first," she said, "and see whether it's marked 'poison' or not." She had never forgotten that, if you drink much from a bottle marked "poison," it is almost certain to disagree with you, sooner or later.

However, this bottle was *not* marked "poison," so Alice ventured to taste it, and finding it very nice (it had a sort of mixed flavor of cherry-tart, custard, pine-apple, roast turkey, toffee, and hot buttered toast), she finished it.

"What a curious feeling!" said Alice. "I must be shutting up like a telescope!"

And so it was indeed: She was now only ten inches high, and her face brightened up at the thought that she was now the right size for going through the little door into that lovely garden.

1. Where does the beginning of the story take place?
Ⓐ in a garden
Ⓑ in a dark hall
Ⓒ in a kitchen
Ⓓ in a rat-hole

2. What is Alice's main problem in the beginning of the story?
Ⓐ She can't decide if she should drink the bottle.
Ⓑ She can't read the label on the bottle.
Ⓒ She is afraid of what's through the doorway.
Ⓓ She is too big to fit through the doorway.

3. Which two words **best** describe Alice?
Ⓐ curious and brave
Ⓑ curious and afraid
Ⓒ careless and afraid
Ⓓ cautious and carefree

4. Why does Alice **most likely** want to get through the door?
Ⓐ She is late for a meeting.
Ⓑ She is too tall.
Ⓒ She is in a dark hall.
Ⓓ She is thirsty.

5. How does Alice begin to solve her problem?
Ⓐ She drinks the bottle labeled "DRINK ME."
Ⓑ She tries to squeeze through the doorway.
Ⓒ She drinks a bottle of poison.
Ⓓ She looks for another way out.

6. How is Alice's problem solved?
Ⓐ She finds a key to another door.
Ⓑ The door gets bigger for her.
Ⓒ She finds another way out.
Ⓓ She drinks the bottle and shrinks.

7. What will probably happen next?
Ⓐ Alice will get bigger again.
Ⓑ Alice will continue to shrink.
Ⓒ Alice will go through the doorway to the garden.
Ⓓ Alice will stay where she is for a while.

8. Why did Alice eventually decide to drink the bottle?
Ⓐ It said "DRINK ME" on it.
Ⓑ It didn't say "poison" on it.
Ⓒ It tasted like roast turkey.
Ⓓ She was very thirsty.

Main Idea and Supporting Details

Read the passage and answer the questions.

Creative Camouflage

In the animal kingdom, it takes creativity to survive. Some animals have developed an amazing technique called camouflage. They can mimic plants, grass, and even other animals in order to hunt or hide.

A leopard's coat helps it surprise and attack its prey. Some leopards have spotted coats, ideal for hiding in the African outback. Others have all-black coats to lurk in the shadows. Monkeys, rabbits, and young buffalo don't stand a chance.

The ornate wobbegongs, or carpet sharks, of Australia and New Guinea flatten their bodies out on the seafloor. Their spots and blotchy lines look like rock and coral. These sharks even have "beards" under their chins that resemble seaweed! Their prey are caught off guard and gobbled up before they know what happened.

Both Arctic owls and polar bears blend in to their snowy environments with their snow-white coverings. The feathers also help keep the owl warm. A polar bear's white fur protects it from other bears and human predators.

The leaf butterflies of Southeast Asia look more like dead leaves than butterflies. They have the coloring of a dead leaf, a fake leaf stalk, and fake leaf veins. Birds assume they are dead leaves and leave the butterflies alone.

Though some animals use camouflage to get food, others use it for safety. These clever disguises help animals survive.

1. What is this passage mainly about?
   - Ⓐ leopards
   - Ⓑ animal camouflage
   - Ⓒ Australian sharks
   - Ⓓ polar bears

2. How does the polar bear's fur help it survive?
   - Ⓐ It helps it blend in so it can attack humans.
   - Ⓑ It helps it blend in so it can hide from humans.
   - Ⓒ It makes it stand out so everyone is afraid.
   - Ⓓ It makes other animals think it is an owl.

3. Why does the leaf butterfly look like a dead leaf?
   - Ⓐ so it can hide in leaves and attack birds
   - Ⓑ so it can lure insects and eat them
   - Ⓒ so it can hide from its predators
   - Ⓓ so it has a place to live in winter

4. Which animal uses camouflage to hunt?
   - Ⓐ leopard
   - Ⓑ rabbit
   - Ⓒ monkey
   - Ⓓ buffalo

5. What is the purpose of paragraph 2?
   - Ⓐ to tell that leopards hunt monkeys and buffalo
   - Ⓑ to show how a leopard's coat helps it hide from predators
   - Ⓒ to show how a leopard's coat helps it sneak up on prey
   - Ⓓ to tell that a leopard lives in the African outback

6. What is the main idea of paragraph 5?
   - Ⓐ Leaf butterflies live in Southeast Asia.
   - Ⓑ Birds hunt leaf butterflies to eat them.
   - Ⓒ Birds don't eat dead leaves they see on the ground.
   - Ⓓ The butterfly looks like a dead leaf to keep it safe.

7. Which animal uses camouflage to wait for its prey to come to it?
   - Ⓐ leopard
   - Ⓑ polar bear
   - Ⓒ rabbit
   - Ⓓ wobbegong

8. What is the main idea of paragraph 4?
   - Ⓐ Arctic owls and polar bears live in cold climates.
   - Ⓑ Arctic owls and polar bears are white to blend in with snow.
   - Ⓒ Arctic owls have feathers.
   - Ⓓ Polar bears have fur.

9. What would be a good supporting detail of the main idea?
   - Ⓐ Bark bugs appear to be part of the tree itself to hide from birds.
   - Ⓑ Male peacocks have colorful feathers to attract a mate.
   - Ⓒ Nearly half the world's chameleon species live in Madagascar.
   - Ⓓ Gaboon vipers are among the most venomous snakes on earth.

10. What is the main idea of the last paragraph?
   - Ⓐ No matter what animals use camouflage for, it helps them survive.
   - Ⓑ Some animals use camouflage for safety.
   - Ⓒ Some animals use camouflage for hunting.
   - Ⓓ All animals have clever ways of disguising themselves to survive.

Distinguishing Facts and Supported Inferences

Read the passage and answer the questions.

Hurricanes

A hurricane is a great, swirling storm that begins over a warm sea. When a hurricane hits land, it can cause enormous damage through violent winds, heavy rain, flooding, and massive waves crashing on the shore.

The word *hurricane* is the regional name for a type of storm known as a *tropical cyclone* when it happens over the North Atlantic Ocean, Caribbean Sea, Gulf of Mexico, or Northeast Pacific Ocean. It would be called a *typhoon* if it occurred in the Northwest Pacific Ocean, west of the international date line. In the Southwest Pacific and Southeast Indian Oceans, it is called a *severe tropical cyclone*, and a *severe cyclonic storm* in the North Indian Ocean. In the Southwest Indian Ocean, such storms are referred to simply as *tropical cyclones*.

Meteorologists are scientists who study the atmosphere. They classify the life of a hurricane in four stages: tropical disturbance, tropical depression, tropical storm, and hurricane.

A tropical disturbance is an area in which rain clouds are building. The clouds can rise to great heights, forming towering thunderclouds. A tropical depression is a low-pressure area surrounded by winds that are moving in a circular pattern, evaporating seawater and feeding more thunderclouds.

Once winds hit 38 miles per hour, it is a tropical storm. The clouds now have a well-defined circular shape. The seas are dangerous. Each tropical storm receives a name to better track it. When winds exceed 74 miles per hour, the storm is upgraded to a hurricane, or the regional equivalent. Hurricanes bring heavy rains, winds, and storm surges.

1. If The Weather Channel reports that a severe cyclonic storm is forming, near which ocean are you located?
   Ⓐ North Atlantic Ocean
   Ⓑ Northwest Pacific Ocean
   Ⓒ North Indian Ocean
   Ⓓ North Pacific Ocean

2. What are storms that have winds of 45 miles per hour called?
   Ⓐ tropical storms
   Ⓑ tropical depressions
   Ⓒ tropical cyclones
   Ⓓ tropical disturbances

3. All tropical storms in the Northwest Pacific Ocean with winds above 74 miles per hour are called _____.
Ⓐ cyclones
Ⓑ typhoons
Ⓒ hurricanes
Ⓓ depressions

4. If a storm has been named, it could be all of the following *except* a _____.
Ⓐ tropical cyclone
Ⓑ tropical depression
Ⓒ hurricane
Ⓓ typhoon

Use the chart below to answer questions 5 and 6. The chart explains how meteorologists classify different strengths of hurricanes.

Hurricane category	Wind speed (mph)	Wind speed (kph)	Storm surge (feet)	Storm surge (meters)	Effects
Category 1 (weak)	74–95	119–153	4–5	1.2–1.5	Minimal damage to trees, shrubbery, and mobile homes
Category 2 (moderate)	96–100	154–177	6–8	1.8–2.4	Considerable damage to trees, mobile homes, and piers; some damage to roofs
Category 3 (strong)	101–130	178–209	9–12	2.7–3.7	Trees blown down or stripped of leaves; mobile homes destroyed; some damages to other buildings
Category 4 (very strong)	131–155	210–249	13–18	4.0–5.5	Extensive damage to windows, doors, and roofs, especially near shore; possible flooding
Category 5 (devasting)	156+	250+	19+	5.8+	Small buildings overturned or blown away; severe structural damage to other buildings

5. What is the weakest hurricane called?
Ⓐ Category 1
Ⓑ Category 2
Ⓒ Category 4
Ⓓ Category 5

6. At which point would trees start being knocked down?
Ⓐ Category 1
Ⓑ Category 2
Ⓒ Category 3
Ⓓ Category 4

Inferences and Conclusions

Read the passage and answer the questions.

The Berlin Wall

The story of the Berlin Wall began as World War II ended. When the Nazis surrendered in 1945, Berlin—the capital of Germany—was a ruined city. In 1949, Western and Eastern Germany formed separate governments.

In the 1950s, more than 3 million people left East Germany for a better life in the West. The Soviet Union knew it had to stop people from leaving. On August 13, 1961, a low, barbed-wire barrier was built between East and West Berlin, dividing the city in half. Later, the barrier was made into a wall 96 miles long and 13 feet high. The government said it was to keep out people from the West, but it really kept people from the East from fleeing. Guards with guns stood watch and shot anyone trying to escape.

People in East Berlin were not happy. The wall kept them from their friends, families, and jobs. Many people tried to leave. About 5,000 people successfully escaped, while 246 people died at the wall.

Protests were held at the wall on the West Berlin side. People painted graffiti and slogans on the wall. In 1987, President Reagan demanded, "Tear down this wall!"

On Friday, November 9, 1989, the people won when the East German government opened its borders, allowing its citizens to visit the West. The world watched the celebrations on television. After 28 years, the Berlin Wall had fallen.

1. Why was Berlin a ruined city in 1945?
   Ⓐ Western Germany ruined it.
   Ⓑ It got ruined from World War II.
   Ⓒ The United States destroyed it.
   Ⓓ Its people all left for other places.

2. Why did 3 million people leave East Germany in the 1950s?
   Ⓐ They didn't like the wall.
   Ⓑ They didn't like the Nazis.
   Ⓒ They wanted a better life.
   Ⓓ They wanted to be communists.

3. How did the East German government deal with so many people leaving East Germany?
   Ⓐ They asked them not to go.
   Ⓑ They asked West Germany for help.
   Ⓒ They ignored it and hoped it would stop.
   Ⓓ They built a wall dividing East and West Berlin.

4. Why did people paint graffiti and slogans on the West Berlin side of the wall?
   Ⓐ They were protesting the Berlin Wall.
   Ⓑ They were showing support for the Berlin Wall.
   Ⓒ They wanted the wall to look pretty.
   Ⓓ President Reagan asked them to.

5. Why were guards with guns on the East Berlin side?
   Ⓐ They kept people from the West out.
   Ⓑ They kept the Nazis out.
   Ⓒ They kept people from escaping.
   Ⓓ They kept the wall safe.

6. Why did 246 people die at the wall?
   Ⓐ The wall was too high for them to climb.
   Ⓑ They were shot by soldiers from the West.
   Ⓒ They died from starvation.
   Ⓓ They were shot by guards for trying to escape.

7. Why was it difficult to escape from East Berlin after the wall was built?
   Ⓐ It wasn't difficult at all to escape.
   Ⓑ Guards in West Berlin stood watch.
   Ⓒ The wall was 96 miles long and stood 13 feet high.
   Ⓓ There were no openings in the wall.

8. Why did people celebrate on November 9, 1989?
   Ⓐ The Berlin Wall was finally torn down.
   Ⓑ It was the 28th anniversary of the wall.
   Ⓒ They were happy that the wall was built.
   Ⓓ It was the anniversary of World War II.

9. What was the reason the East German government gave for building the Berlin Wall?
   Ⓐ They wanted to keep people from escaping to the West.
   Ⓑ They wanted to keep out people from the West.
   Ⓒ They wanted to keep the Nazis from regaining power.
   Ⓓ They wanted to make East Germany safer for democracy.

10. What was one negative effect the Berlin Wall had on people in West Berlin?
    Ⓐ They were trapped by the wall in West Berlin.
    Ⓑ They couldn't paint graffiti on the wall on their side.
    Ⓒ They had to climb the wall to get to work in East Berlin.
    Ⓓ They had friends and family stuck on the other side.

Interpreting Poems

Read the excerpt of the poem and answer the questions.

Rain in Summer

excerpt by Henry Wadsworth Longfellow

1 How beautiful is the rain!
2 After the dust and heat,
3 In the broad and fiery street,
4 In the narrow lane,
5 How beautiful is the rain!

6 How it clatters along the roofs,
7 Like the tramp of hoofs
8 How it gushes and struggles out
9 From the throat of the overflowing spout!

10 Across the window-pane
11 It pours and pours;
12 And swift and wide,
13 With a muddy tide,
14 Like a river down the gutter roars
15 The rain, the welcome rain!

16 In the country, on every side,
17 Where far and wide,
18 Like a leopard's tawny and spotted hide,
19 Stretches the plain,
20 To the dry grass and the drier grain
21 How welcome is the rain!

1. Why does the author **most likely** use the term *fiery street?*
   Ⓐ to show how the streets were on fire
   Ⓑ to show how hot it was before the rain
   Ⓒ to frighten the reader with images of fire
   Ⓓ to describe the color of the streets

2. What thought is repeated throughout the poem?
   Ⓐ The rain is welcome.
   Ⓑ The leopard has spots.
   Ⓒ The rain is making mud.
   Ⓓ It is summertime.

3. When does this poem take place?
   Ⓐ winter
   Ⓑ spring
   Ⓒ summer
   Ⓓ fall

4. What literary device does the author use over and over?
   Ⓐ onomatopoeia
   Ⓑ simile
   Ⓒ alliteration
   Ⓓ hyperbole

5. How does the author organize this poem?
   Ⓐ in paragraphs
   Ⓑ in chronological order
   Ⓒ in order of importance
   Ⓓ in stanzas

6. How does the author **most likely** feel about the rain?
   Ⓐ happy
   Ⓑ sad
   Ⓒ annoyed
   Ⓓ frightened

7. The author compares the rain to all of these except _____.
   Ⓐ clattering hoofs
   Ⓑ a leopard's spotty hide
   Ⓒ a roaring river
   Ⓓ the grass and grain

8. What does the author use *like the tramp of hoofs* to describe?
   Ⓐ how the rain looks
   Ⓑ how the rain sounds
   Ⓒ how the rain feels
   Ⓓ how the rain smells

9. From whose point of view is this poem told?
   Ⓐ an observer
   Ⓑ the rain
   Ⓒ a leopard
   Ⓓ the land

10. What is the rhyme scheme in the last stanza?
    Ⓐ A-B-A-B-A-B
    Ⓑ A-A-B-B-A-A
    Ⓒ A-A-A-B-B-B
    Ⓓ A-B-B-A-B-B

Understanding Informational Texts

Read the passage and answer the questions.

Tropical Rain Forests

Tropical rain forests are the oldest and most diverse ecosystem on earth. Today, tropical rain forests cover only 6 percent of the earth's ground surface, but they are home to more than half of the planet's animal and plant species.

The rain forest is made up of four layers: the forest floor, the understory, the canopy, and the emergent layer. The forest floor is on the bottom. It is a carpet of dead leaves, ferns, mosses, and mushrooms. The understory is 0–60 feet above ground, and hardly any sun reaches here. Most plants and animals live in the canopy, which is 60–130 feet above ground. The emergent layer is 130–160 feet above the ground, with the tallest trees reaching almost 200 feet.

More than 25 percent of our medicines come from rain forest plants, and these plants make up only a tiny fraction of rain forest species. Fruits, vegetables, nuts, coffee, chocolate, vanilla, oils, wood, and rubber all come from the rain forest.

Scientists believe that until about 10,000 years ago, the world had 6 billion acres of tropical rain forest. By 1950, we had around 2.8 billion acres of rain forest. Today, roughly 1.5 acres of rain forest are destroyed every second, and we have less than 1.5 billion acres left. If we don't do something, in just 30 years there will be very little tropical rain forest left.

1. Look at the time line to the right. How many acres of rain forest were left in 1950?
Ⓐ 6 billion acres
Ⓑ 2.8 billion acres
Ⓒ 1.5 billion acres
Ⓓ 1.5 acres

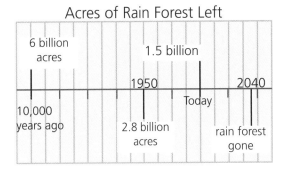

Acres of Rain Forest Left

Louis is filling in this picture of the layers of a tropical rain forest. Use it to answer questions 2 and 3.

2. Where should he put *canopy*?
Ⓐ Layer 1
Ⓑ Layer 2
Ⓒ Layer 3
Ⓓ Layer 4

3. Which layer has the ferns and mosses?
Ⓐ Layer 1
Ⓑ Layer 2
Ⓒ Layer 3
Ⓓ Layer 4

4. How does the author organize paragraph 2?
Ⓐ chronologically
Ⓑ in order from bottom to top
Ⓒ in order from top to bottom
Ⓓ by comparing and contrasting

5. What would be a good heading to put before paragraph 2?
Ⓐ The Rain Forest in Danger
Ⓑ Life in the Canopy
Ⓒ Layers of the Rain Forest
Ⓓ Products of the Rain Forest

6. Which does **not** come from the rain forest?
Ⓐ coffee
Ⓑ vanilla
Ⓒ rubber
Ⓓ plastic

Determining Word Meanings

Choose the word or words that help you understand the meaning of the underlined word in each sentence.

1. James enjoys reading books about <u>marsupials</u>, especially kangaroos.
Ⓐ James
Ⓑ reading
Ⓒ books
Ⓓ kangaroos

2. The campers put their food in a <u>cache</u>—a hiding place—to keep it safe from animals.
Ⓐ campers
Ⓑ food
Ⓒ hiding place
Ⓓ animals

3. Some types of sugar, like <u>glucose</u>, are found naturally in fruits.
Ⓐ sugar
Ⓑ found
Ⓒ naturally
Ⓓ fruits

4. A <u>vista</u>—a distant view—of the mountains and pine trees opened before us.
Ⓐ distant view
Ⓑ mountains
Ⓒ pine trees
Ⓓ opened

Choose the base word for each word.

5. impossible
Ⓐ im
Ⓑ possible
Ⓒ ible
Ⓓ imposs

6. unthinkable
Ⓐ un
Ⓑ unthink
Ⓒ think
Ⓓ able

7. wonderful
Ⓐ won
Ⓑ der
Ⓒ ful
Ⓓ wonder

8. heartless
Ⓐ heart
Ⓑ art
Ⓒ less
Ⓓ artless

9. misleading
Ⓐ mis
Ⓑ lead
Ⓒ ing
Ⓓ slead

10. requirement
Ⓐ re
Ⓑ quire
Ⓒ require
Ⓓ ment

Choose the correct answer.

11. Which word comes from the Greek root
ast, meaning *star?*
Ⓐ astronomy
Ⓑ blasting
Ⓒ castaway
Ⓓ fastener

12. Which word comes from the Latin root
ped, meaning *foot?*
Ⓐ hopped
Ⓑ centipede
Ⓒ impede
Ⓓ sloped

13. Which word comes from the Latin root
loc, meaning *place?*
Ⓐ warlock
Ⓑ clockwise
Ⓒ location
Ⓓ velocity

14. Which word comes from the Latin root
mit, meaning *send?*
Ⓐ transmit
Ⓑ mitten
Ⓒ blacksmith
Ⓓ limit

15. Which word comes from the Latin root
don, meaning *give?*
Ⓐ London
Ⓑ abandon
Ⓒ donut
Ⓓ donate

16. The prefix *mis–* in *misbehave* means
_____.
Ⓐ not
Ⓑ again
Ⓒ full of
Ⓓ bad

17. The suffix *–en* in *sharpen* means
_____.
Ⓐ in
Ⓑ make
Ⓒ one who
Ⓓ not

18. In which word does *able* mean the same
as it does in *acceptable?*
Ⓐ fable
Ⓑ cables
Ⓒ washable
Ⓓ tablet

19. Which suffix means *state of?*
Ⓐ -ment
Ⓑ -ous
Ⓒ dis-
Ⓓ un-

20. Which prefix means *again?*
Ⓐ dis-
Ⓑ re-
Ⓒ -or
Ⓓ -er

Using Context Clues

Read the passage and fill in the missing words. Choose the word that sounds best in each sentence.

Sherman Poppen is most often ___(1)___ with inventing the snowboard in 1965. ___(2)___ , he put two skis together for his daughter to surf down a snowy slope outside their home. Combining the words snow and surf, the new invention became the Snurfer. It went into ___(3)___ in 1966.

Over the next decade, early ___(4)___ created more ___(5)___ board designs. By the early 1980s, a handful of snowboard brands were in stores.

Snowboarding became ___(6)___ in the mid-1980s. Since mostly teenage boys snowboarded, a rebel reputation was ___(7)___ . It still ___(8)___ today, in spite of snowboarding's huge ___(9)___ to men and women of all ages.

Some ski resorts ___(10)___ snowboarding during this early phase but have since come to accept the wildly popular and still growing winter sport. In the year 2000, snowboarding was the fastest-growing sport in the United States, with more than 7.2 million people snowboarding. In 1998, snowboarding first made an ___(11)___ in the Olympics in Nagano, Japan, with a giant slalom and halfpipe competition. It returned to the 2006 Olympics in Torino, Italy, with the ___(12)___ of a snowboard cross.

1. Ⓐ credited
    Ⓑ accused
    Ⓒ invented
    Ⓓ interested

2. Ⓐ Importantly
    Ⓑ Unfortunately
    Ⓒ Supposedly
    Ⓓ Gradually

3. Ⓐ hiding
    Ⓑ production
    Ⓒ invention
    Ⓓ discovery

4. Ⓐ opposers
    Ⓑ settlers
    Ⓒ critics
    Ⓓ pioneers

5. Ⓐ rebellious
    Ⓑ refined
    Ⓒ red
    Ⓓ random

6. Ⓐ boring
    Ⓑ popular
    Ⓒ scarce
    Ⓓ hopeful

7. Ⓐ abandoned
    Ⓑ discovered
    Ⓒ established
    Ⓓ neglected

8. Ⓐ disappears
    Ⓑ fails
    Ⓒ succeeds
    Ⓓ prevails

9. Ⓐ appeal
    Ⓑ turnoff
    Ⓒ application
    Ⓓ disgust

10. Ⓐ welcomed
    Ⓑ instituted
    Ⓒ banned
    Ⓓ allowed

11. Ⓐ exhibit
    Ⓑ appearance
    Ⓒ exit
    Ⓓ outlet

12. Ⓐ satisfaction
    Ⓑ eloquence
    Ⓒ calculation
    Ⓓ addition

Section 2: Written and Oral Language Conventions

Audience, Purpose, and Format

Read each paragraph and answer the questions that follow.

> My fifth-grade class is learning about local farming and agriculture. We would like to come visit your farm and discover what the day-to-day activities of running a farm entail. Would you be open to having us plan a field trip to your farm? We would like to come sometime next month. Please let us know if this is possible.

1. What is the appropriate format for this writing?
   Ⓐ an essay
   Ⓑ a report
   Ⓒ a letter
   Ⓓ a short story

2. Who would be an appropriate person to send this to?
   Ⓐ the school principal
   Ⓑ a teacher
   Ⓒ the mayor
   Ⓓ a local farmer

3. What other information should be included?
   Ⓐ what crops the class is learning about
   Ⓑ how many students will be attending
   Ⓒ the class's teacher's name
   Ⓓ what month next month is

4. Why was this paragraph written?
   Ⓐ to tell what the author is learning in school
   Ⓑ to inform about local agriculture
   Ⓒ to request a place to have a field trip
   Ⓓ to persuade people to own farms

> Australia is home to many interesting animals. Among them are the Tasmanian devil, platypus, bandicoot, and quokka. These unusual animals are indigenous to Australia and have unique features.

5. This paragraph would **best** be part of
   _____.
   Ⓐ a poem
   Ⓑ a letter
   Ⓒ a fiction story
   Ⓓ a report

6. Who would be the **best** audience for this paragraph?
   Ⓐ an Australian citizen
   Ⓑ a teacher
   Ⓒ a relative
   Ⓓ a business owner

I recently found out that the city plans to tear down the 34th Street Park because it needs too many repairs. I am writing to express my disappointment. That park has been a place for children to play for the past 50 years. My grandmother played in that park when she was a little girl. It should not be torn down. Instead, there are things that can be done to improve it so it can be enjoyed for many years to come.

7. Who should this letter be sent to?
Ⓐ the mayor
Ⓑ a teacher
Ⓒ a relative
Ⓓ a friend

8. Why is this letter being written?
Ⓐ to persuade the reader to destroy the park
Ⓑ to persuade the reader to save the 34th Street Park
Ⓒ to inform the reader about the author's grandmother
Ⓓ to entertain the reader with stories about the park

A long time ago, there was a man who lived in a small town with his wife and children. The family did not have much money, but they did have a special tree that grew in their backyard. They called this tree "The Wishing Tree." It granted any wish that a person made while sitting under it, as long as the wish was not greedy or selfish.

9. What is the **best** format for this writing?
Ⓐ an essay
Ⓑ a poem
Ⓒ a fictional narrative
Ⓓ a book report

10. Why did the author probably write this paragraph?
Ⓐ to inform readers about the man and his family
Ⓑ to entertain readers with an interesting story
Ⓒ to warn readers about being greedy and selfish
Ⓓ to convince readers to get a wishing tree

Prewriting and Composing

Read each paragraph and answer the questions that follow.

Jolene just won first place for her apple pie in the baking contest at her county fair. She is writing a letter to her grandmother to tell her about the exciting experience.

1. Which of these strategies will **best** help Jolene plan her letter?
   Ⓐ eating a piece of the apple pie that won
   Ⓑ reading a cookbook for apple pie recipes
   Ⓒ reviewing the form of a business letter
   Ⓓ recalling the events that led to her winning

2. What details should Jolene include in her letter?
   Ⓐ the types of apples she likes to eat
   Ⓑ the names of the other contestants
   Ⓒ what she did to get ready for the contest
   Ⓓ what other things happened at the fair

3. Which of these should Jolene start her letter with?
   Ⓐ Dear Grandma,
   Ⓑ To whom it may concern:
   Ⓒ To my grandmother
   Ⓓ Dear Mrs. Gabriel,

4. Which of these would be a good first sentence?
   Ⓐ I got an A on my last math test!
   Ⓑ I have exciting news to tell you.
   Ⓒ Homemade apple pie is tasty.
   Ⓓ I used green and red apples.

5. Which sentence should **not** be included in Jolene's letter?
   Ⓐ I followed the recipe that you gave me.
   Ⓑ There is a good movie on TV tonight.
   Ⓒ I picked the apples myself at the orchard.
   Ⓓ I made the lattice the way you showed me.

Pedro's teacher has asked each student to write an essay. The essay topic is the different ways the school can help the environment.

6. Which of these would **best** help Pedro plan his essay?
   Ⓐ thinking of things that are in the environment
   Ⓑ asking the teacher for a narrower topic
   Ⓒ asking his parents for help in writing the essay
   Ⓓ making a list of things that the school can do

7. What would be a good topic sentence for Pedro to start his essay with?
   Ⓐ There are many ways that our school can help the environment.
   Ⓑ Recycling helps the environment by reducing the amount of garbage.
   Ⓒ We can start a recycling program easily.
   Ⓓ Every little bit that we do helps.

Pedro made this outline to help organize his ideas. Use it to answer questions 8–12.

I. Ways to Help the Environment
II. Recycle
   A. Put recycling bins in the cafeteria.
      1. Have one for plastic.
      2. Have one for glass.
   B. Reduce the use of disposables in the cafeteria.
   C. Put bins in each classroom for paper.
III. Save Electricity
   A.
   B. Install sensors that turn lights on and off.
   C. Change the lightbulbs to energy-efficient.
IV. Save Water
   A. Install faucets that turn off on their own.

8. Which of these could Pedro add under III. A.?
   Ⓐ Add air conditioners in every room.
   Ⓑ Keep the lights on all day.
   Ⓒ Turn the lights off when you leave a room.
   Ⓓ Wear coats all day instead of turning on the heat.

9. Which line should be under a different heading?
   Ⓐ Put recycling bins in the cafeteria.
   Ⓑ Reduce the use of disposables in the cafeteria.
   Ⓒ Install faucets that turn off on their own.
   Ⓓ Put bins in each classroom for paper.

10. What transition can Pedro use when he goes from talking about recycling to saving electricity?
   Ⓐ First, we can save electricity in the school.
   Ⓑ Another way we can help is by saving electricity.
   Ⓒ But we can save electricity.
   Ⓓ Lastly, we can save electricity.

11. Which would **not** be a good sentence for Pedro to include in his essay?
   Ⓐ I like the food in the cafeteria.
   Ⓑ Energy-efficient lightbulbs use less electricity and save money.
   Ⓒ A lot of water is wasted when kids wash their hands.
   Ⓓ We go through a lot of paper in the classroom.

12. What is the **best** format for Pedro's essay?
   Ⓐ rhyming verses
   Ⓑ numbered sentences
   Ⓒ dialogues
   Ⓓ paragraphs

Research and Technology

Jacob is writing a research report about green sea turtles. He is in the library doing research.
Answer the questions about Jacob's research.

1. Jacob wants to say, "Each green sea turtle has distinctive facial markings, <u>like</u> fingerprints." He looked up *like* in the thesaurus. Which synonym for *like* would **best** fit his sentence?
   - Ⓐ enjoy
   - Ⓑ prefer
   - Ⓒ similar to
   - Ⓓ fancy

2. Jacob found a book called *Sea Turtles in Danger*. In what part of the book would he **most likely** find the titles of other books about green sea turtles?
   - Ⓐ the copyright page
   - Ⓑ the bibliography
   - Ⓒ the glossary
   - Ⓓ the table of contents

3. What topic should Jacob look under in the encyclopedia to find out more about green sea turtle habitats?
   - Ⓐ turtle
   - Ⓑ green
   - Ⓒ sea
   - Ⓓ habitat

4. What would be the **best** key words for Jacob to use to search the Internet for more information about green sea turtles being an endangered species?
   - Ⓐ turtle species
   - Ⓑ green sea
   - Ⓒ endangered green
   - Ⓓ endangered sea turtles

5. Where is the **best** place for Jacob to look for more information about where green sea turtles live?
   - Ⓐ a book about animals
   - Ⓑ a magazine about beaches
   - Ⓒ a dictionary
   - Ⓓ an atlas

6. Jacob found a library book about Hawaiian wildlife. Where should he look to see if the book has information about sea turtles?
   - Ⓐ the title page
   - Ⓑ the index
   - Ⓒ the glossary
   - Ⓓ the copyright page

Use this dictionary entry to answer questions 7 and 8.

flip·per (flip′er) *n.* **1.** A wide flat limb, as of an aquatic animal, adapted for swimming: *The seal flapped his flippers at us.* **2.** A rubber covering for the foot, used in swimming and diving: *The divers put on flippers to help them swim.* **3.** A flat lever in a pinball machine, used to hit the ball so it stays in play: *I hit the flippers to hit the pinball.*

7. In his first draft, Jacob wrote this sentence:
Sea turtles' body shape and paddle-shaped flippers make them swift swimmers.
Which definition of *flipper* **best** fits the way Jacob used it in his sentence?
Ⓐ 1
Ⓑ 2
Ⓒ 3
Ⓓ none

8. How should Jacob divide *flippers* at the end of a line?
Ⓐ flipp-ers
Ⓑ fli-ppers
Ⓒ flip-pers
Ⓓ flipper-s

Use this table of contents from the book *Sea Turtles: The Complete Guide* to answer questions 9 and 10.

1	Introduction	1
2	Life Cycles	10
3	Biology	30
4	History	52
5	Conservation	70
6	Green Turtles	84
7	Loggerheads	125
8	Flatbacks	149
9	Leatherbacks	169
10	Conclusion	201
	Index	225

9. Which chapter should Jacob look in to find the turtle he's doing his report on?
Ⓐ 6
Ⓑ 7
Ⓒ 8
Ⓓ 9

10. On which page should Jacob start looking for information about what's being done to protect the endangered sea turtles?
Ⓐ 10
Ⓑ 30
Ⓒ 52
Ⓓ 70

Revising

Read the essay that Lisa wrote and answer the questions that follow.

Summer Vacation

(1) My family and I are trying to decide where to go on vacation for two weeks. (2) My brother wants to go camping at a lake he likes to fish. (3) He likes adventure movies. (4) My sister wants to go to New York City and sea the Statue of Liberty. (5) I want to go to the beach where I can sit in the sun and read books. (6) My father has always wanted to go to the Appalachian Mountains. (7) And go hiking there. (8) My mother just wants to go somewhere she can shop? (9) We can't agree on where we should go. (10) We only have a few more days before they have to make the plans.

1. What sentence should be taken out?
- Ⓐ sentence 3
- Ⓑ sentence 4
- Ⓒ sentence 7
- Ⓓ sentence 8

2. What is the **best** way to combine sentences 6 and 7 without changing their meaning?
- Ⓐ My father has always wanted to go to the Appalachian Mountains hiking.
- Ⓑ My father has always wanted to go to the Appalachian Mountains and go hiking there.
- Ⓒ My father has always wanted to go hiking in the Appalachian Mountains.
- Ⓓ My father has always wanted to go to the Appalachian Mountains, to go hiking.

3. What is the **best** way to write sentence 2?
- Ⓐ My brother wants to go camping at a lake, and he likes to fish.
- Ⓑ My brother wants to go camping at a lake because he likes to fish.
- Ⓒ My brother wants to go camping at a lake, he likes to fish.
- Ⓓ correct as is

4. What is the **best** way to write sentence 8?
- Ⓐ My mother just wants to go somewhere, she can shop?
- Ⓑ My mother just wants to go somewhere she can shop.
- Ⓒ My mother just wants to go, somewhere she can shop!
- Ⓓ correct as is

5. What is the **best** place for sentence 9?
- Ⓐ after sentence 1
- Ⓑ after sentence 4
- Ⓒ after sentence 7
- Ⓓ correct as is

6. Where is the **best** place for a comma in sentence 5?
- Ⓐ I, want to go to the beach where I can sit in the sun and read books.
- Ⓑ I want to go to the beach where I can sit in the sun, and read books.
- Ⓒ I want to go to the beach where, I can sit in the sun and read books.
- Ⓓ I want to go to the beach, where I can sit in the sun and read books.

7. Which sentence has a spelling error?
- Ⓐ sentence 2
- Ⓑ sentence 4
- Ⓒ sentence 6
- Ⓓ sentence 8

8. What sentence could **best** be added at the end of the paragraph?
- Ⓐ Vacations are fun and relaxing.
- Ⓑ My friend is also planning a vacation.
- Ⓒ I hope we can agree on something soon!
- Ⓓ We have no school in the summer.

9. Which sentence is **not** a complete thought?
- Ⓐ sentence 1
- Ⓑ sentence 3
- Ⓒ sentence 5
- Ⓓ sentence 7

10. Which sentence has a pronoun used incorrectly?
- Ⓐ sentence 2
- Ⓑ sentence 8
- Ⓒ sentence 9
- Ⓓ sentence 10

Sentence Construction

Read the journal entry that Nolan wrote and answer the questions.

January 27

(1) Today was my parents' wedding anniversary. (2) My sister Katie and I wanted to do something special for them. (3) First, we were careful not to wake them when we got up. (4) We crept downstairs and made them breakfast. (5) Katie made the bacon, and I made the eggs. (6) Then we put it all on a tray and brought it to the bedroom. (7) We gave them breakfast in bed. (8) They really enjoyed. (9) After breakfast, we all watched their wedding video and looked at wedding pictures. (10) My mother looked so beautiful in her wedding dress! (11) They went out to dinner tonight. (12) We stayed with our grandmother.

1. What is the dependent clause in sentence 3?
- Ⓐ we were careful
- Ⓑ we were
- Ⓒ when we got up
- Ⓓ we got up

2. What is the independent clause in sentence 9?
- Ⓐ After breakfast
- Ⓑ the wedding video
- Ⓒ looked at wedding pictures
- Ⓓ we all watched their wedding video

3. What word **best** combines sentences 11 and 12?

Ⓐ yet

Ⓑ so

Ⓒ because

Ⓓ since

4. Which sentence is incomplete?

Ⓐ sentence 8

Ⓑ sentence 6

Ⓒ sentence 3

Ⓓ sentence 1

5. Which sentence shows an example of an appositive?

Ⓐ sentence 2

Ⓑ sentence 4

Ⓒ sentence 7

Ⓓ sentence 9

6. Which sentence is a compound sentence?

Ⓐ sentence 2

Ⓑ sentence 3

Ⓒ sentence 5

Ⓓ sentence 6

7. What kind of sentence is sentence 10?

Ⓐ declarative

Ⓑ interrogative

Ⓒ imperative

Ⓓ exclamatory

8. Which sentence has a compound subject?

Ⓐ sentence 2

Ⓑ sentence 4

Ⓒ sentence 7

Ⓓ sentence 9

Choose the answer that is a complete and correctly written sentence.

9. Ⓐ I has made dinner and will serve it at six.

Ⓑ I ran to the bus stop, and still missed the bus?

Ⓒ The plot was realistic, but the acting was bad.

Ⓓ I studied for my math test it is tomorrow.

10. Ⓐ The hare took a nap, but the tortoise crept slow on.

Ⓑ He found a coded message and figured out the code.

Ⓒ I will takes the bus or walked to school tomorrow.

Ⓓ The doctor examines the patient, the nurse assisted.

Grammar

Choose the best way to write the underlined words in each sentence. Remember, the best way to write it may be the way it is already written.

1. <u>My sister and me</u> went to a piano recital last night.
   Ⓐ Me and my sister
   Ⓑ My sister and I
   Ⓒ I and my sister
   Ⓓ correct as is

2. The class <u>are</u> going on a field trip to the zoo tomorrow.
   Ⓐ was
   Ⓑ be
   Ⓒ is
   Ⓓ correct as is

3. My grandmother let me borrow <u>she's</u> pearl necklace for the dance.
   Ⓐ her
   Ⓑ hers
   Ⓒ she
   Ⓓ correct as is

4. Last night I <u>tried</u> Mexican food for the first time.
   Ⓐ try
   Ⓑ trying
   Ⓒ have tired
   Ⓓ correct as is

5. The water <u>is dripped</u> in the bathroom sink upstairs.
   Ⓐ dripping
   Ⓑ is dripping
   Ⓒ drip
   Ⓓ correct as is

6. Close the windows <u>behind</u> the storm.
   Ⓐ against
   Ⓑ without
   Ⓒ during
   Ⓓ correct as is

7. Tonight I have math homework <u>and</u> history homework.
   Ⓐ or
   Ⓑ but
   Ⓒ because
   Ⓓ correct as is

8. Birch leaves turn yellow, <u>so</u> maple leaves turn red.
   Ⓐ but
   Ⓑ or
   Ⓒ since
   Ⓓ correct as is

9. The wind was so strong yesterday that it <u>blowed</u> down a branch from the oak tree.
Ⓐ blown
Ⓑ blew
Ⓒ blows
Ⓓ correct as is

10. Many writers <u>have wrote</u> tales of Pecos Bill, the legendary cowboy.
Ⓐ have write
Ⓑ has written
Ⓒ have written
Ⓓ correct as is

11. Roberto carried his trumpet with <u>her</u> on the plane.
Ⓐ him
Ⓑ his
Ⓒ them
Ⓓ correct as is

12. <u>Them</u> took a trip to Italy last summer with the Italian club.
Ⓐ Us
Ⓑ Me
Ⓒ They
Ⓓ correct as is

13. Which is <u>biggest</u>, an elephant or a blue whale?
Ⓐ bigger
Ⓑ most big
Ⓒ more big
Ⓓ correct as is

14. I just played the <u>worse</u> tennis game of my life.
Ⓐ more bad
Ⓑ most bad
Ⓒ worst
Ⓓ correct as is

15. In the spring, flowers <u>were</u> growing where I planted the bulbs last fall.
Ⓐ was
Ⓑ am
Ⓒ had
Ⓓ correct as is

16. What will <u>happening</u> when Molly has her puppies?
Ⓐ happens
Ⓑ happen
Ⓒ happened
Ⓓ correct as is

17. James has <u>did</u> a report on the solar system.
Ⓐ done
Ⓑ do
Ⓒ does
Ⓓ correct as is

18. You should drive <u>more careful</u> in the rain than when it is sunny.
Ⓐ more carefully
Ⓑ most careful
Ⓒ most carefully
Ⓓ correct as is

Mechanics

Choose which underlined part in each sentence contains an error in capitalization or punctuation.
If there is no mistake in the sentence, choose the *No mistake* option.

1. Yesterday i drew a picture of Sam playing baseball. No mistake
    Ⓐ   Ⓑ   Ⓒ   Ⓓ

2. We joined the Spanish Club in september. No mistake
    Ⓐ   Ⓑ   Ⓒ   Ⓓ

3. "Blake do you want some pizza?" asked Jill. No mistake
    Ⓐ   Ⓑ   Ⓒ   Ⓓ

4. Weve been practicing for the recital since Sunday. No mistake
    Ⓐ   Ⓑ   Ⓒ   Ⓓ

5. I am going to Scotts house for dinner tonight. No mistake
    Ⓐ   Ⓑ   Ⓒ   Ⓓ

6. The senator will meet you at 7:00 PM tomorrow. No mistake
       Ⓐ   Ⓑ   Ⓒ   Ⓓ

7. My mother's favorite song is "A Kiss to Build a dream On." No mistake
      Ⓐ   Ⓑ   Ⓒ   Ⓓ

8. Hurricane Katrina hit Louisiana on August 29 2005. No mistake
    Ⓐ   Ⓑ   Ⓒ   Ⓓ

9. The largest U.S. state is Alaska and the smallest state is Rhode Island. No mistake
        Ⓐ   Ⓑ   Ⓒ   Ⓓ

10. Mrs Winterson assigned the class a report on the poem "The Bells." No mistake
    Ⓐ   Ⓑ   Ⓒ   Ⓓ

11. Casey, a ten-year-old boy, won the spelling bee this year. No mistake
    Ⓐ   Ⓑ   Ⓒ   Ⓓ

12. Did you know that my father visited Japan last summer. No mistake
      Ⓐ   Ⓑ   Ⓒ   Ⓓ

Choose the answer that shows the correct way to write the underlined part in each sentence.

13. Michelle can speak <u>French, german and Spanish</u>.
    Ⓐ French, German and Spanish
    Ⓑ French, German, and Spanish
    Ⓒ french, german, and Spanish
    Ⓓ French, german and Spanish

14. Chris asked, <u>"have you seen my keys."</u>
    Ⓐ "Have you seen my keys?"
    Ⓑ "Have you seen my keys."
    Ⓒ "have you seen my keys?"
    Ⓓ "have you seen my keys."

15. The captain blew the <u>whistle. And</u> steered the ship from the dock.
    Ⓐ whistle, and
    Ⓑ whistle; and
    Ⓒ whistle. And
    Ⓓ whistle and

16. <u>Yes mr</u> Jones is away on vacation this week.
    Ⓐ Yes Mr.
    Ⓑ Yes, Mr.
    Ⓒ Yes, Mr
    Ⓓ Yes mr

17. Next summer we are going to <u>San francisco California</u>.
    Ⓐ San Francisco California
    Ⓑ San francisco, California
    Ⓒ San Francisco, California
    Ⓓ San francisco California

18. The doctor said, <u>eat more vegetables.</u>
    Ⓐ "eat more vegetables."
    Ⓑ "Eat more vegetables."
    Ⓒ Eat more vegetables.
    Ⓓ eat more vegetables.

19. The bus picks me up in the morning at <u>730</u>.
    Ⓐ 7:30
    Ⓑ 7-30
    Ⓒ 7/30
    Ⓓ 730

20. If you go to the store, I need the <u>following eggs bread,</u> and milk.
    Ⓐ following, eggs, bread,
    Ⓑ following: eggs bread
    Ⓒ following: eggs, bread,
    Ⓓ following eggs bread,

Spelling

Choose the word in each sentence that is not spelled correctly. If there is no misspelling in the sentence, choose the *No mistake* option.

1. She <u>received</u> her <u>aceptance</u> letter to <u>science</u> camp yesterday. <u>No mistake</u>
     Ⓐ   Ⓑ   Ⓒ   Ⓓ

2. The trip was the <u>perfect</u> <u>apertunity</u> for him to see <u>Arizona</u>. <u>No mistake</u>
        Ⓐ   Ⓑ   Ⓒ   Ⓓ

3. We will <u>probably</u> have <u>frozen</u> pizza for <u>dinner</u>. <u>No mistake</u>
         Ⓐ   Ⓑ   Ⓒ   Ⓓ

4. Dan helped Mrs. Jones with her <u>grocerie</u> <u>shopping</u> on the <u>weekends</u>. <u>No mistake</u>
                Ⓐ   Ⓑ   Ⓒ   Ⓓ

5. Mr. Klein was very <u>particular</u> about the <u>upkeep</u> of his <u>gardens</u>. <u>No mistake</u>
          Ⓐ   Ⓑ   Ⓒ   Ⓓ

6. People are <u>suposed</u> to get plenty of <u>exercise</u> to stay <u>healthy</u>. <u>No mistake</u>
            Ⓐ   Ⓑ   Ⓒ   Ⓓ

7. They found <u>dinosaur</u> <u>fossills</u> <u>buried</u> in their backyard. <u>No mistake</u>
             Ⓐ   Ⓑ   Ⓒ   Ⓓ

8. The <u>two</u> brothers always <u>quareled</u> over the <u>computer</u>. <u>No mistake</u>
        Ⓐ   Ⓑ   Ⓒ   Ⓓ

9. The <u>calender</u> listed all the <u>appointments</u> the <u>doctor</u> had. <u>No mistake</u>
         Ⓐ   Ⓑ   Ⓒ   Ⓓ

10. Paula <u>threw</u> a party to <u>celabrate</u> her parents' <u>anniversary</u>. <u>No mistake</u>
           Ⓐ   Ⓑ   Ⓒ   Ⓓ

11. Someone must have eaten all the leftover dessert. No mistake
     (A)   (B)   (C)   (D)

12. We were able to see the sun rize over the mountains. No mistake
          (A)   (B)   (C)   (D)

13. Its good weather to go swimming in the lake. No mistake
   (A)   (B)   (C)   (D)

14. I rote a letter to the editor of the newspaper. No mistake
   (A)   (B)   (C)   (D)

Choose the word that is spelled correctly.

15. (A) purchased
    (B) perchised
    (C) purchised
    (D) perchused

16. (A) rehursing
    (B) reharsing
    (C) rehersing
    (D) rehearsing

17. (A) tensun
    (B) tensian
    (C) tension
    (D) tenshun

18. (A) primative
    (B) primetive
    (C) premative
    (D) primitive

19. (A) accident
    (B) acident
    (C) accidant
    (D) acidant

20. (A) faverite
    (B) favorit
    (C) favorite
    (D) faveritte

Vocabulary

Choose the correct synonym for each word.

1. powerful
- Ⓐ strong
- Ⓑ coarse
- Ⓒ normal
- Ⓓ huge

2. quantity
- Ⓐ lots
- Ⓑ few
- Ⓒ amount
- Ⓓ several

3. thankful
- Ⓐ graceful
- Ⓑ generous
- Ⓒ glorious
- Ⓓ grateful

4. normal
- Ⓐ organized
- Ⓑ average
- Ⓒ different
- Ⓓ similar

5. tidy
- Ⓐ neat
- Ⓑ small
- Ⓒ empty
- Ⓓ mighty

6. enraged
- Ⓐ happy
- Ⓑ pleased
- Ⓒ careless
- Ⓓ angry

Choose the correct antonym for each word.

7. drenched
- Ⓐ moist
- Ⓑ dry
- Ⓒ soaked
- Ⓓ damp

8. expensive
- Ⓐ pay
- Ⓑ cheap
- Ⓒ costly
- Ⓓ afford

9. rapid
- Ⓐ quick
- Ⓑ river
- Ⓒ slow
- Ⓓ coarse

10. demolish
- Ⓐ taste
- Ⓑ destroy
- Ⓒ throw
- Ⓓ build

11. cautious
- Ⓐ careful
- Ⓑ careless
- Ⓒ respected
- Ⓓ painful

12. interfere
- Ⓐ hinder
- Ⓑ enter
- Ⓒ finish
- Ⓓ ignore

Choose the correct meaning for each underlined word.

13. Janene was <u>absent</u> from class today.
Ⓐ late
Ⓑ early
Ⓒ quiet
Ⓓ missing

14. I was able to <u>obtain</u> two free tickets for the concert.
Ⓐ get
Ⓑ buy
Ⓒ sell
Ⓓ pick

15. We are having the <u>annual</u> New Year's Eve party at our house this year.
Ⓐ daily
Ⓑ usual
Ⓒ fancy
Ⓓ yearly

16. Because we like pizza, we <u>frequently</u> eat it for lunch or dinner.
Ⓐ never
Ⓑ often
Ⓒ rarely
Ⓓ seldom

17. After walking around the city all day, I'm feeling a bit <u>exhausted</u>.
Ⓐ excited
Ⓑ bored
Ⓒ tired
Ⓓ refreshed

18. Though the show was sold out, there were <u>vacant</u> seats in the theater.
Ⓐ crowded
Ⓑ filled
Ⓒ wooden
Ⓓ empty

19. For Miriam's birthday her mom planned a <u>casual</u> backyard barbecue.
Ⓐ fancy
Ⓑ relaxed
Ⓒ occasional
Ⓓ accidental

20. We hung a <u>portrait</u> of Aunt Penelope in the hall.
Ⓐ dress
Ⓑ memory
Ⓒ mirror
Ⓓ picture

21. I stared at my test grade in <u>disbelief</u>.
Ⓐ understanding
Ⓑ surprise
Ⓒ doubt
Ⓓ happiness

22. Marcus was <u>elected</u> to be class president.
Ⓐ chosen
Ⓑ called
Ⓒ rejected
Ⓓ preferred

Section 3: Test

Read the passage and answer the questions.

Seven Wonders of the Ancient World

The seven wonders of the ancient world are a group of man-made objects that are considered notable because they are very large or have some other unusual quality. They were all built between about 2500 and 250 BCE.

The pyramids of Egypt at Giza are the oldest and the best preserved of all the ancient wonders. The largest pyramid, called the Great Pyramid, stands about 450 feet high.

The Hanging Gardens of Babylon were probably built between 605 and 562 BCE. The gardens were about 75 feet above the ground. Water from the Euphrates River was used to water the lush gardens.

The Temple of Artemis at Ephesus, built about 550 BCE, was one of the largest and most sophisticated temples built in ancient times. It burned down in 356 BCE.

The 43-foot-high statue of Zeus at Olympia, Greece, had a robe of gold. There is much debate over what happened to the statue. Many believe that a fire destroyed it in 462 CE. Others believe it was taken to Constantinople and lost to a fire that destroyed the city in 475 CE.

The Mausoleum at Halicarnassus was a 150-foot-high marble tomb, built about 353 BCE to hold the remains of Mausolus. An earthquake in the 1200s CE brought it to pieces.

The Colossus of Rhodes was a 110-foot-tall bronze statue that stood near the harbor of Rhodes. It was built between 294 and 282 BCE. In 226 BCE, it was knocked down by an earthquake.

The Lighthouse of Alexandria, which was more than 440 feet high, stood for about 1,500 years in the harbor of Alexandria, Egypt. It was built during the reign of Ptolemy II (283–246 BCE), and was toppled by an earthquake.

1. Why did the author write about the seven wonders of the ancient world?
  Ⓐ to entertain with stories of yore
  Ⓑ to inform about a piece of history
  Ⓒ to persuade people to visit them
  Ⓓ to explain how they were built

2. Which structure was **not** destroyed by an earthquake?
  Ⓐ the Temple of Artemis at Ephesus
  Ⓑ the Mausoleum at Halicarnassus
  Ⓒ the Colossus of Rhodes
  Ⓓ the Lighthouse of Alexandria

3. Which of the seven wonders still exists today?
  Ⓐ the Colossus of Rhodes
  Ⓑ the statue of Zeus
  Ⓒ the pyramids of Egypt
  Ⓓ the Hanging Gardens of Babylon

4. What is this passage mainly about?
  Ⓐ places that tourists should see
  Ⓑ how earthquakes destroy
  Ⓒ gods of the ancient world
  Ⓓ ancient wonders of the world

5. How does the author organize this passage?
  Ⓐ by using cause and effect
  Ⓑ in order from tallest to shortest
  Ⓒ by comparing and contrasting each object
  Ⓓ in chronological order from oldest to newest

6. Read this sentence from the passage.
  It was built during the reign of Ptolemy II (283–246 BCE). What does *reign* mean here?
  Ⓐ time in power
  Ⓑ precipitation
  Ⓒ a strap to control an animal
  Ⓓ takedown of a leader

Look at the map below. Use it to answer questions 7 and 8.

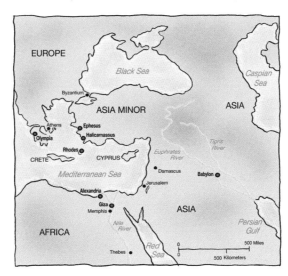

7. Which wonder was set farthest from the others?
  Ⓐ the Colossus of Rhodes
  Ⓑ the pyramids at Giza
  Ⓒ the Hanging Gardens of Babylon
  Ⓓ the Lighthouse of Alexandria

8. Which wonder was in present-day Europe?
  Ⓐ the Hanging Gardens of Babylon
  Ⓑ the Statue of Zeus
  Ⓒ the Temple of Artemis at Ephesus
  Ⓓ the Mausoleum at Halicarnassus

Matthew is writing a letter to his cousin about spring break. Read his first draft below and answer the questions.

Dear Liz,

(1) I cant believe its almost spring brake already. (2) I am so excited? (3) It will be so good to see you again. (4) It will be so good to spend time with you again. (5) We families will has fun on vacation together. (6) I want to go to the amusement park ride the roller coaster and eat cotton candy. (7) My Brother and me are all packed. (8) Our plane leaves next Wednesday afternoon. (9) The dog will go to the kennel, and the cat will be fed by a neighbor. (10) Everything is almost ready for the big trip. (11) Last year we went to Florida. (12) I'm glad your sister will be there too. (13) We don't get to see her much since she went away to college. (14) Well, I better get going. (15) We will see. (16) You on Wednesday!

Sincerely,
Matthew

9. How is sentence 1 **best** written?
- Ⓐ I can't believe its almost spring break already.
- Ⓑ I can't believe it's almost spring brake already.
- Ⓒ I can't believe it's almost spring break already.
- Ⓓ correct as is

10. How is sentence 2 **best** written?
- Ⓐ I am so excited.
- Ⓑ I am so excited!
- Ⓒ I am, so excited.
- Ⓓ correct as is

11. How can sentences 3 and 4 **best** be combined without changing their meaning?
- Ⓐ It will be so good to see you and spend time with you again.
- Ⓑ It will be so good to see you again and spend time with you again.
- Ⓒ It will be so good to see you, and to spend time with you.
- Ⓓ It will be so good to see you again; to spend time with you.

12. What is the **best** way to write sentence 5?
- Ⓐ We families will have fun on vacation together.
- Ⓑ Us families will has fun on vacation together.
- Ⓒ Our families will have fun on vacation together.
- Ⓓ correct as is

13. What punctuation is missing from sentence 6?

Ⓐ periods

Ⓑ colons

Ⓒ semicolons

Ⓓ commas

14. How should sentence 7 be written?

Ⓐ My brother and I are all packed.

Ⓑ Me and my brother are all packed.

Ⓒ My Brother and I are all packed.

Ⓓ correct as is

15. How should sentence 8 be written?

Ⓐ Our plane leaves next wednesday afternoon.

Ⓑ Our plain leaves next Wednesday afternoon.

Ⓒ Our plane leaves, next Wednesday, afternoon.

Ⓓ correct as is

16. What kind of sentence is sentence 9?

Ⓐ complex

Ⓑ compound

Ⓒ simple

Ⓓ run-on

17. If Matthew wants to find a synonym for *big* in sentence 10, where should he look?

Ⓐ the dictionary

Ⓑ an encyclopedia

Ⓒ a thesaurus

Ⓓ a newspaper

18. Which sentence doesn't belong in Matthew's letter?

Ⓐ sentence 11

Ⓑ sentence 12

Ⓒ sentence 13

Ⓓ sentence 14

19. Which sentence is an incomplete thought?

Ⓐ sentence 9

Ⓑ sentence 11

Ⓒ sentence 13

Ⓓ sentence 16

20. Where would be the **best** place to add the following sentence?

We arrive at 3:00.

Ⓐ after sentence 6

Ⓑ after sentence 8

Ⓒ after sentence 10

Ⓓ after sentence 12

Section 4: Number Sense

Place Value

Answer the questions below.

1. What is the value of the underlined digit in 147,<u>6</u>09?
- Ⓐ 60
- Ⓑ 600
- Ⓒ 6,000
- Ⓓ 60,000

2. What digit is in the tens place of 237,586?
- Ⓐ 3
- Ⓑ 5
- Ⓒ 7
- Ⓓ 8

3. What is the correct way to write five hundred seventy six thousand, four hundred thirty in digits?
- Ⓐ 500,76,000,400,30
- Ⓑ 50,076,430
- Ⓒ 576,430
- Ⓓ 57,6430

4. What place is the 4 in 435,629?
- Ⓐ hundreds
- Ⓑ thousands
- Ⓒ ten thousands
- Ⓓ hundred thousands

5. What digit is in the next highest place value from the hundreds in 9,382,467?
- Ⓐ 2
- Ⓑ 3
- Ⓒ 4
- Ⓓ 6

6. What is the expanded form of 422,507?
- Ⓐ 40,000 + 2,000 + 500 + 7
- Ⓑ 400,000 + 20,000 + 2,000 + 500 + 70
- Ⓒ 40,000 + 22,000 + 500 + 70
- Ⓓ 400,000 + 20,000 + 2,000 + 500 + 7

7. What is the correct way to write 9,236,578 in words?
- Ⓐ nine hundred thousand, two hundred thirty-six thousand, five hundred seventy-eight
- Ⓑ nine hundred thousand two hundred, thirty-six thousand five hundred, seventy-eight
- Ⓒ nine million, two hundred thirty-six thousand, five hundred seventy-eight
- Ⓓ nine million two hundred, thirty-six thousand five hundred, seventy-eight

8. What is the correct way to write 27,482 in words?
- Ⓐ twenty-seven thousand four hundred, eighty-two
- Ⓑ twenty-seven thousand, four hundred eighty-two
- Ⓒ two hundred seven thousand four hundred, eighty-two
- Ⓓ two hundred seven thousand, four hundred eighty-two

9. What is the correct way to write five hundred ten thousand, two hundred eighty in digits with proper commas?
- Ⓐ 510,280
- Ⓑ 5,10,280
- Ⓒ 500,010,280
- Ⓓ 5,000,10,280

Rounding

Answer the questions below. Remember, to round a number you should look at the digit in the next place. Round up if it is 5 or more. Round down if it is 4 or less.

1. Round 543,634 to the nearest thousand.
Ⓐ 544,000
Ⓑ 543,600
Ⓒ 543,000
Ⓓ 540,000

2. Round six hundred twenty-two thousand, four hundred two to the nearest ten thousand.
Ⓐ 600,000
Ⓑ 620,000
Ⓒ 622,000
Ⓓ 622,400

3. Round 947 to the nearest ten.
Ⓐ 9,000
Ⓑ 947
Ⓒ 950
Ⓓ 1,000

4. Round 398,205 to the nearest thousand.
Ⓐ 0
Ⓑ 398,000
Ⓒ 400,000
Ⓓ 1,000,000

5. Round four million, thirty two thousand, four hundred sixty-eight to the nearest thousand.
Ⓐ 4,000,000
Ⓑ 4,032,000
Ⓒ 4,032,500
Ⓓ 4,033,000

6. Round 473,689.0173 to the nearest thousandth.
Ⓐ 474,000
Ⓑ 473,689.02
Ⓒ 473,689.017
Ⓓ 473,000

7. Round seven hundred ninety thousand, four hundred seven and three hundred sixty-seven ten thousandths to the nearest hundredth.
Ⓐ 790,407
Ⓑ 790,407.037
Ⓒ 790,407.04
Ⓓ 790,410

8. Round 4,269,493 to the nearest thousand.
Ⓐ 4,300,000
Ⓑ 4,270,000
Ⓒ 4,269,000
Ⓓ 4,000,000

9. Round 312,592 to the nearest ten thousand.
Ⓐ 300,000
Ⓑ 310,000
Ⓒ 312,600
Ⓓ 313,000

10. Which place would you have rounded 298,340 to if your answer was 298,000?
Ⓐ hundreds
Ⓑ thousands
Ⓒ ten thousands
Ⓓ hundred thousands

11. Round 249 to the nearest hundred.
Ⓐ 0
Ⓑ 200
Ⓒ 250
Ⓓ 1,000

12. Which place would you have rounded 12,458,409 to if your answer was 12,500,000?
Ⓐ ten millions
Ⓑ millions
Ⓒ hundred thousands
Ⓓ ten thousands

Estimating

Estimate the sums or differences. Remember, to estimate you should first round each number to the same place value. Then solve each problem using the rounded numbers.

1. 3,780 + 3,480 =
Ⓐ 6,000
Ⓑ 7,000
Ⓒ 8,000
Ⓓ 9,000

2. .00395820 + .00953713 =
Ⓐ .012
Ⓑ .013
Ⓒ .014
Ⓓ .015

3. 3,472,793 − 2,748,391 =
Ⓐ 1,000,000
Ⓑ 900,000
Ⓒ 800,000
Ⓓ 700,000

4. .07843 − .03827 =
Ⓐ .04
Ⓑ .03
Ⓒ .02
Ⓓ .01

5. 23,593,685 + 96,257,194 =
Ⓐ 121,000,000
Ⓑ 120,000,000
Ⓒ 119,000,000
Ⓓ 118,000,000

6. 8,557 − 2,806 =
Ⓐ 5,600
Ⓑ 5,700
Ⓒ 5,800
Ⓓ 5,900

7. 334,263 − 232,200 =
Ⓐ 105,000
Ⓑ 100,000
Ⓒ 200,000
Ⓓ 120,000

8. 25,390 + 98,653 =
Ⓐ 124,000
Ⓑ 120,000
Ⓒ 121,000
Ⓓ 123,000

9. 3,783,897 + 8,893,332 =
Ⓐ 16,000,000
Ⓑ 15,000,000
Ⓒ 14,000,000
Ⓓ 13,000,000

10. .009287338 − .007389220 =
Ⓐ .002
Ⓑ .003
Ⓒ .004
Ⓓ .005

11. 5,567 + 7,109 =
Ⓐ 12,800
Ⓑ 12,700
Ⓒ 12,600
Ⓓ 12,500

12. 67,340 − 26,342 =
Ⓐ 39,000
Ⓑ 40,000
Ⓒ 41,000
Ⓓ 14,000

Estimate the products or quotients.

13. 810 × 206 =
Ⓐ 240,000
Ⓑ 16,000
Ⓒ 24,000
Ⓓ 160,000

14. .00113 × .0073 =
Ⓐ .000073
Ⓑ .000007
Ⓒ .00001
Ⓓ .00073

15. 4,327 × 6,683 =
Ⓐ 28,000,000
Ⓑ 2,400,000
Ⓒ 30,000,000
Ⓓ 3,500,000

16. 63,870 ÷ 895 =
Ⓐ 63
Ⓑ 67
Ⓒ 71
Ⓓ 75

17. .0036 ÷ .00086 =
Ⓐ 4.44444
Ⓑ 3.6
Ⓒ .36
Ⓓ 4

18. .0417 ÷ .0063 =
Ⓐ 7
Ⓑ 6.95
Ⓒ 6
Ⓓ 5.96

19. 5,234 × 7,893 =
Ⓐ 30,000,000
Ⓑ 35,000,000
Ⓒ 40,000,000
Ⓓ 45,000,000

20. 25,430 ÷ 5,487 =
Ⓐ 4
Ⓑ 5
Ⓒ 6
Ⓓ 7

21. 81,004 ÷ 93 =
Ⓐ 600
Ⓑ 700
Ⓒ 800
Ⓓ 900

22. 789 × 984 =
Ⓐ 800,000
Ⓑ 700,000
Ⓒ 600,000
Ⓓ 500,000

23. 360,035 ÷ 610 =
Ⓐ 600
Ⓑ 700
Ⓒ 800
Ⓓ 900

24. .0009342 ÷ .0003224 =
Ⓐ 2
Ⓑ 3
Ⓒ 4
Ⓓ 5

Adding and Subtracting Whole Numbers

Find the sum or difference for each problem.

1. 25,458
 − 14,484

- Ⓐ 10,974
- Ⓑ 10,074
- Ⓒ 11,974
- Ⓓ 11,074

2. 83,362
 + 4,433

- Ⓐ 86,795
- Ⓑ 87,695
- Ⓒ 87,795
- Ⓓ 87,785

3. 1,356
 + 463

- Ⓐ 1,719
- Ⓑ 1,819
- Ⓒ 1,810
- Ⓓ 1,710

4. 2,565
 +1,923

- Ⓐ 3,488
- Ⓑ 4,588
- Ⓒ 3,588
- Ⓓ 4,488

5. 55,138
 − 48,452

- Ⓐ 6,686
- Ⓑ 7,686
- Ⓒ 7,786
- Ⓓ 17,786

6. 395,678
 − 183,973

- Ⓐ 212,705
- Ⓑ 311,705
- Ⓒ 312,705
- Ⓓ 211,705

7. 657,882
 + 287,720

- Ⓐ 945,602
- Ⓑ 954,602
- Ⓒ 940,602
- Ⓓ 450,902

8. 328,561
 + 835,273

- Ⓐ 163,834
- Ⓑ 1,160,834
- Ⓒ 1,163,834
- Ⓓ 1,260,834

9. 734,559
 − 348,920

- Ⓐ 380,639
- Ⓑ 385,639
- Ⓒ 358,639
- Ⓓ 385,693

10. 439,213
 + 872,894

- Ⓐ 312,107
- Ⓑ 321,107
- Ⓒ 1,321,107
- Ⓓ 1,312,107

11. 142,647
 + 392,642

- Ⓐ 435,289
- Ⓑ 535,289
- Ⓒ 534,892
- Ⓓ 434,289

12. 116,968
 − 66,981

- Ⓐ 49,879
- Ⓑ 50,987
- Ⓒ 49,987
- Ⓓ 49,798

13. 37,234 – 19,526 =
  (A) 18,708
  (B) 17,708
  (C) 28,718
  (D) 27,708

14. 748,287 – 359,293 =
  (A) 499,094
  (B) 488,994
  (C) 388,994
  (D) 399,094

15. 894,367 + 782,889 =
  (A) 1,667,256
  (B) 1,677,256
  (C) 1,677,652
  (D) 1,766,256

16. 672,892 – 456,208 =
  (A) 216,684
  (B) 261,648
  (C) 261,842
  (D) 246,864

17. 652,778 + 289,008 =
  (A) 942,768
  (B) 841,786
  (C) 941,687
  (D) 941,786

18. 783,020 – 342,561 =
  (A) 440,549
  (B) 404,459
  (C) 440,459
  (D) 441,954

19. 889,564 – 334,578 =
  (A) 554,896
  (B) 554,698
  (C) 555,086
  (D) 554,986

20. 674,284 + 889,342 =
  (A) 1,563,626
  (B) 1,541,626
  (C) 1,563,226
  (D) 1,536,662

21. 485 + 323 + 573 =
  (A) 1,371
  (B) 1,281
  (C) 1,271
  (D) 1,381

22. 17,353 + 4,936 =
  (A) 22,289
  (B) 21,289
  (C) 23,389
  (D) 23,289

Mental Math

Mental math is used to calculate math problems in your head. Use mental math strategies to find the value of the variable.

1. $37 + g = 37$
  Ⓐ 0
  Ⓑ 1
  Ⓒ 37
  Ⓓ 2

2. $14 + 9 + 6 = s$
  Ⓐ 19
  Ⓑ 27
  Ⓒ 29
  Ⓓ 39

3. $(7 + 32) + 13 = x$
  Ⓐ 42
  Ⓑ 52
  Ⓒ 53
  Ⓓ 63

4. $63 - a = 63$
  Ⓐ 0
  Ⓑ 1
  Ⓒ 2
  Ⓓ 63

5. $31 - 8 - 2 = r$
  Ⓐ 11
  Ⓑ 21
  Ⓒ 24
  Ⓓ 37

6. $z - 19 - 21 = 5$
  Ⓐ 21
  Ⓑ 31
  Ⓒ 35
  Ⓓ 45

7. $j \times 13 = 13 \times 6$
  Ⓐ 5
  Ⓑ 6
  Ⓒ 7
  Ⓓ 8

8. $3 \times (6 \times 7) = (3 \times 6) \times k$
  Ⓐ 7
  Ⓑ 6
  Ⓒ 5
  Ⓓ 3

9. $132 \times v = 132$
  Ⓐ 0
  Ⓑ 1
  Ⓒ 2
  Ⓓ 132

10. $t \div 1 = 745$
  Ⓐ 0
  Ⓑ 1
  Ⓒ 745
  Ⓓ 845

11. $35 \div p = 5$
  Ⓐ 5
  Ⓑ 6
  Ⓒ 7
  Ⓓ 8

12. $0 \div 41 = w$
  Ⓐ 41
  Ⓑ 3
  Ⓒ 1
  Ⓓ 0

Dividing

Divide to find each quotient.

1. 1,620 ÷ 2 =
- Ⓐ 610
- Ⓑ 660
- Ⓒ 810
- Ⓓ 840

2. 1,533 ÷ 3 =
- Ⓐ 511
- Ⓑ 475
- Ⓒ 462
- Ⓓ 431

3. 2,384 ÷ 8 =
- Ⓐ 264
- Ⓑ 298
- Ⓒ 316
- Ⓓ 386

4. 4)3,448
- Ⓐ 662
- Ⓑ 686
- Ⓒ 862
- Ⓓ 886

5. 7)2,513
- Ⓐ 359
- Ⓑ 249
- Ⓒ 479
- Ⓓ 521

6. 6)2,826
- Ⓐ 356
- Ⓑ 387
- Ⓒ 432
- Ⓓ 471

7. 3,570 ÷ 15 =
- Ⓐ 214
- Ⓑ 238
- Ⓒ 278
- Ⓓ 324

8. 13,472 ÷ 16 =
- Ⓐ 721
- Ⓑ 775
- Ⓒ 816
- Ⓓ 842

9. 7,898 ÷ 22 =
- Ⓐ 234
- Ⓑ 296
- Ⓒ 359
- Ⓓ 427

10. 33)17,886
- Ⓐ 542
- Ⓑ 584
- Ⓒ 622
- Ⓓ 442

11. 47)10,199
- Ⓐ 117
- Ⓑ 217
- Ⓒ 237
- Ⓓ 337

12. 79)50,955
- Ⓐ 545
- Ⓑ 575
- Ⓒ 645
- Ⓓ 675

Factors and Multiples

Answer the questions below.

1. Which number is 24 divisible by?
Ⓐ 5
Ⓑ 7
Ⓒ 8
Ⓓ 9

2. Which number is 38 divisible by?
Ⓐ 2
Ⓑ 3
Ⓒ 4
Ⓓ 5

3. Which number is 48 **not** divisible by?
Ⓐ 12
Ⓑ 28
Ⓒ 8
Ⓓ 4

4. Which number is 12 **not** divisible by?
Ⓐ 3
Ⓑ 4
Ⓒ 6
Ⓓ 8

5. Which number is **not** a factor of 16?
Ⓐ 9
Ⓑ 8
Ⓒ 4
Ⓓ 2

6. Which number is **not** a factor of 33?
Ⓐ 1
Ⓑ 3
Ⓒ 11
Ⓓ 22

7. What is the greatest common factor of 8 and 12?
Ⓐ 2
Ⓑ 4
Ⓒ 12
Ⓓ 24

8. What is the greatest common factor of 20 and 34?
Ⓐ 6
Ⓑ 4
Ⓒ 2
Ⓓ 1

9. Which number is a multiple of 6?
Ⓐ 2
Ⓑ 4
Ⓒ 8
Ⓓ 12

10. Which number is a multiple of 10?
Ⓐ 5
Ⓑ 15
Ⓒ 20
Ⓓ 25

11. What is the least common multiple of 6 and 8?
Ⓐ 24
Ⓑ 28
Ⓒ 48
Ⓓ 52

12. What is the least common multiple of 5 and 7?
Ⓐ 15
Ⓑ 35
Ⓒ 45
Ⓓ 70

Equivalent Fractions

Answer the questions below.

1. Which fraction is equivalent to $\frac{1}{3}$?

Ⓐ $\frac{3}{12}$

Ⓑ $\frac{9}{24}$

Ⓒ $\frac{3}{9}$

Ⓓ $\frac{3}{7}$

2. Which fraction is equivalent to $\frac{12}{18}$?

Ⓐ $\frac{2}{3}$

Ⓑ $\frac{3}{4}$

Ⓒ $\frac{24}{46}$

Ⓓ $\frac{5}{6}$

3. Which fraction is **not** equivalent to $\frac{2}{5}$?

Ⓐ $\frac{4}{10}$

Ⓑ $\frac{8}{18}$

Ⓒ $\frac{10}{25}$

Ⓓ $\frac{6}{15}$

4. Which fraction is **not** equivalent to $\frac{6}{8}$?

Ⓐ $\frac{3}{4}$

Ⓑ $\frac{18}{24}$

Ⓒ $\frac{12}{18}$

Ⓓ $\frac{30}{40}$

5. Which number makes $\frac{3}{x} = \frac{9}{18}$ a true statement?

Ⓐ 3

Ⓑ 6

Ⓒ 4

Ⓓ 5

6. Which fraction is equivalent to $\frac{4}{7}$?

Ⓐ $\frac{12}{22}$

Ⓑ $\frac{8}{15}$

Ⓒ $\frac{24}{43}$

Ⓓ $\frac{16}{28}$

7. Which fraction is equivalent to $\frac{13}{52}$?

Ⓐ $\frac{1}{4}$

Ⓑ $\frac{28}{104}$

Ⓒ $\frac{39}{154}$

Ⓓ $\frac{1}{3}$

8. Which fraction is **not** equivalent to $\frac{1}{2}$?

Ⓐ $\frac{13}{26}$

Ⓑ $\frac{4}{8}$

Ⓒ $\frac{8}{14}$

Ⓓ $\frac{27}{54}$

9. Which fraction is **not** equivalent to $\frac{16}{48}$?

Ⓐ $\frac{8}{24}$

Ⓑ $\frac{4}{12}$

Ⓒ $\frac{1}{3}$

Ⓓ $\frac{2}{8}$

10. Which number makes $\frac{x}{7} = \frac{20}{28}$ a true statement?

Ⓐ 4

Ⓑ 6

Ⓒ 3

Ⓓ 5

11. Which number makes $\frac{2}{5} = \frac{x}{35}$ a true statement?

Ⓐ 10

Ⓑ 14

Ⓒ 16

Ⓓ 12

12. Which number makes $\frac{7}{12} = \frac{49}{x}$ a true statement?

Ⓐ 84

Ⓑ 72

Ⓒ 74

Ⓓ 96

Adding and Subtracting Fractions

Answer the questions below. Reduce all fractions to the simplest form.

1. $\frac{3}{7} + \frac{2}{7} =$

(A) $\frac{5}{7}$

(B) $\frac{5}{14}$

(C) $\frac{1}{7}$

(D) $\frac{1}{14}$

2. $\frac{8}{9} - \frac{3}{9} =$

(A) $\frac{5}{0}$

(B) $\frac{5}{9}$

(C) $\frac{5}{18}$

(D) 0

3. $\frac{6}{13} + \frac{4}{13} =$

(A) $\frac{2}{13}$

(B) $\frac{5}{13}$

(C) $\frac{10}{26}$

(D) $\frac{10}{13}$

4. $\frac{3}{5} - \frac{1}{5} =$

(A) $\frac{1}{5}$

(B) $\frac{2}{10}$

(C) $\frac{2}{5}$

(D) 0

5. $\frac{3}{4} + \frac{1}{8} =$

(A) $\frac{4}{12}$

(B) $\frac{7}{8}$

(C) $\frac{8}{8}$

(D) $\frac{1}{3}$

6. $\frac{3}{10} - \frac{1}{5} =$

(A) $\frac{1}{10}$

(B) $\frac{2}{5}$

(C) $\frac{1}{5}$

(D) $\frac{2}{10}$

7. $\frac{5}{9} + \frac{1}{3} =$

(A) $\frac{6}{9}$

(B) $\frac{6}{12}$

(C) $\frac{8}{9}$

(D) $\frac{1}{2}$

8. $\frac{2}{3} - \frac{7}{12} =$

(A) $\frac{1}{3}$

(B) $\frac{3}{12}$

(C) 0

(D) $\frac{1}{12}$

9. $\frac{1}{4} + \frac{2}{6} =$

(A) $\frac{7}{12}$

(B) $\frac{3}{10}$

(C) $\frac{3}{4}$

(D) $\frac{1}{2}$

10. $\frac{2}{3} - \frac{1}{5} =$

(A) $\frac{1}{3}$

(B) $\frac{7}{15}$

(C) $\frac{1}{5}$

(D) $\frac{2}{5}$

11. $\frac{2}{7} + \frac{3}{5} =$

(A) $\frac{5}{12}$

(B) $\frac{5}{6}$

(C) $\frac{31}{35}$

(D) $\frac{29}{35}$

12. $\frac{5}{8} - \frac{1}{3} =$

(A) $\frac{7}{24}$

(B) $\frac{4}{5}$

(C) $\frac{1}{2}$

(D) $\frac{5}{16}$

Multiplying and Dividing Fractions and Mixed Numbers

Answer the questions below. Answers should be in simplest form.

1. $\frac{2}{3} \times \frac{1}{4} =$

Ⓐ $\frac{1}{6}$

Ⓑ $\frac{2}{12}$

Ⓒ $\frac{3}{7}$

Ⓓ 2

2. $\frac{3}{5} \div \frac{1}{7} =$

Ⓐ $\frac{5}{21}$

Ⓑ $4\frac{1}{5}$

Ⓒ $\frac{21}{5}$

Ⓓ $\frac{3}{35}$

3. $\frac{4}{8} \times \frac{2}{9} =$

Ⓐ $\frac{8}{72}$

Ⓑ $2\frac{1}{4}$

Ⓒ $\frac{1}{9}$

Ⓓ $\frac{2}{18}$

4. $\frac{5}{13} \div \frac{7}{11} =$

Ⓐ $\frac{91}{55}$

Ⓑ $\frac{55}{91}$

Ⓒ $1\frac{36}{55}$

Ⓓ $\frac{35}{143}$

5. $\frac{4}{5} \times 3 =$

Ⓐ $2\frac{2}{5}$

Ⓑ $\frac{12}{15}$

Ⓒ $\frac{4}{15}$

Ⓓ $\frac{12}{5}$

6. $\frac{1}{2} \div 7 =$

Ⓐ $\frac{7}{14}$

Ⓑ $3\frac{1}{2}$

Ⓒ $\frac{7}{2}$

Ⓓ $\frac{1}{14}$

7. $8 \times \frac{5}{11} =$

Ⓐ $\frac{40}{11}$

Ⓑ $\frac{40}{88}$

Ⓒ $3\frac{7}{11}$

Ⓓ $\frac{5}{88}$

8. $5 \div \frac{3}{6} =$

Ⓐ $\frac{2}{5}$

Ⓑ 10

Ⓒ $2\frac{1}{2}$

Ⓓ $\frac{30}{3}$

9. $\frac{1}{11} \times 3\frac{2}{3} =$

Ⓐ $\frac{1}{3}$

Ⓑ $3\frac{2}{33}$

Ⓒ $\frac{11}{33}$

Ⓓ $\frac{2}{3}$

10. $\frac{3}{4} \div 1\frac{4}{5} =$

Ⓐ $\frac{27}{20}$

Ⓑ $2\frac{2}{5}$

Ⓒ $\frac{5}{12}$

Ⓓ $\frac{12}{5}$

11. $5\frac{3}{7} \times \frac{1}{2} =$

Ⓐ $5\frac{3}{14}$

Ⓑ $\frac{19}{7}$

Ⓒ $2\frac{3}{14}$

Ⓓ $2\frac{5}{7}$

12. $4\frac{2}{5} \div \frac{3}{8} =$

Ⓐ $\frac{15}{176}$

Ⓑ $5\frac{1}{15}$

Ⓒ $\frac{176}{15}$

Ⓓ $11\frac{11}{15}$

Decimals

Answer the questions below. Round up or down when needed.

1. Which decimal is equivalent to the fraction $\frac{3}{4}$?
Ⓐ 75.0
Ⓑ 7.5
Ⓒ .75
Ⓓ .075

2. Which fraction is equivalent to the decimal $.66\bar{6}$?
Ⓐ $\frac{3}{4}$
Ⓑ $\frac{1}{3}$
Ⓒ $\frac{1}{4}$
Ⓓ $\frac{2}{3}$

3. What is 2.46 × 3.29?
Ⓐ .8193
Ⓑ 8.0934
Ⓒ 80.934
Ⓓ 80934

4. What is the correct way to read 234.0324?
Ⓐ two hundred thirty-four and three hundred twenty-four thousandths
Ⓑ two hundred thirty-four and three hundred twenty-four ten thousandths
Ⓒ two hundred thirty four thousand, three hundred twenty-four ten thousandths
Ⓓ two hundred thirty-four thousand, three hundred twenty-four thousandths

5. Which shows the decimals in order from greatest to least?
Ⓐ .7, .08, .009, .0010
Ⓑ .0010, .009, .08, .7
Ⓒ .1, .01, .001, .011
Ⓓ .011, .001, .01, .1

6. What is the correct way to read .00293?
Ⓐ two hundred ninety three
Ⓑ two hundred ninety three thousandths
Ⓒ two hundred ninety three ten thousandths
Ⓓ two hundred ninety three hundred thousandths

7. What is 5.4 × 6.49?
Ⓐ 35.05
Ⓑ 3.51
Ⓒ .35
Ⓓ .04

8. Which is the proper way to write three hundred seventy-two thousandths as a decimal?
Ⓐ .00372
Ⓑ .0372
Ⓒ .372
Ⓓ 3.72

9. Which shows the decimals in order from least to greatest?
Ⓐ .35, 3.5, 35.0, 350
Ⓑ 258, 25.8, 2.58, .258
Ⓒ .12, 1.2, 120, 12.0
Ⓓ 2.43, 243, 24.3, .243

10. What is 304.5 ÷ .4032?
- Ⓐ 7,552.08
- Ⓑ 755.21
- Ⓒ 75.52
- Ⓓ 7.55

11. What is 22.492 + 1.03201?
- Ⓐ 2.352
- Ⓑ 12.57
- Ⓒ 23.52
- Ⓓ 125.69

12. What is .0275 − .017?
- Ⓐ .0105
- Ⓑ .0258
- Ⓒ .105
- Ⓓ .258

13. What decimal is equivalent to $\frac{1}{7}$?
- Ⓐ .014
- Ⓑ .14
- Ⓒ 1.4
- Ⓓ 14.0

14. Which of the following decimals is $\frac{327}{1,000}$?
- Ⓐ .0327
- Ⓑ .327
- Ⓒ 3.27
- Ⓓ 32.7

15. Which of the following fractions is .45?
- Ⓐ $\frac{45}{10,000}$
- Ⓑ $\frac{45}{1,000}$
- Ⓒ $\frac{45}{100}$
- Ⓓ $\frac{45}{10}$

16. Which fraction is equivalent to $0.16\overline{66}$?
- Ⓐ $\frac{1}{8}$
- Ⓑ $\frac{1}{6}$
- Ⓒ $\frac{3}{12}$
- Ⓓ $\frac{3}{4}$

17. Which of the following decimals is $\frac{43,204}{10,000}$?
- Ⓐ .043204
- Ⓑ .43204
- Ⓒ 4.3204
- Ⓓ 43.204

18. Which of the following fractions is 1.0321?
- Ⓐ $\frac{10,321}{10,000}$
- Ⓑ $\frac{10,321}{1,000}$
- Ⓒ $\frac{100,321}{10,000}$
- Ⓓ $\frac{100,321}{1,000}$

19. Which of the following mixed numbers is the same as 4.25?
- Ⓐ $\frac{34}{8}$
- Ⓑ $4\frac{2}{8}$
- Ⓒ $4\frac{2}{4}$
- Ⓓ $\frac{18}{4}$

20. Which of the following decimals is the same as $3\frac{6}{8}$?
- Ⓐ 3.68
- Ⓑ .368
- Ⓒ 3.75
- Ⓓ .375

21. Which of the following mixed numbers is larger than 3.50?
- Ⓐ $3\frac{2}{8}$
- Ⓑ $3\frac{3}{8}$
- Ⓒ $3\frac{1}{6}$
- Ⓓ $3\frac{6}{10}$

Percentages

Answer the questions below.

1. What is 30% of 100?
Ⓐ .03
Ⓑ .3
Ⓒ 3
Ⓓ 30

2. What is 20% of 300?
Ⓐ 60
Ⓑ 200
Ⓒ 2,000
Ⓓ 6,000

3. What percent of 450 is 90?
Ⓐ 5%
Ⓑ 20%
Ⓒ 405%
Ⓓ 500%

4. What is 47% of 3,682 rounded to the nearest hundred?
Ⓐ 1,700
Ⓑ 1,730
Ⓒ 1,730.5
Ⓓ 1,731

5. 356 is what percent of 6,349 rounded to the nearest tenth?
Ⓐ .1%
Ⓑ 5.6%
Ⓒ 56.1%
Ⓓ 57%

6. .74 is the same as which of the following?
Ⓐ .74%
Ⓑ 7.4%
Ⓒ 74%
Ⓓ 740%

7. The distance between Molly's house and Jim's house is about 138 miles. If Jim gets 85% of the way to Molly's house before running out of gas, how much farther does he need to travel to get to Molly's house?
Ⓐ 117.3 miles
Ⓑ 96.6 miles
Ⓒ 41.4 miles
Ⓓ 20.7 miles

8. Christina was counting her stamp collection when she dropped some of the stamps on the floor. If she had 76 stamps, and she dropped 25% of them, how many stamps are on the floor?
Ⓐ 57 stamps
Ⓑ 38 stamps
Ⓒ 27 stamps
Ⓓ 19 stamps

9. Adam wants to purchase a concert ticket online. The ticket costs $47.50 plus a 9% service fee. How much does the ticket cost him altogether?
Ⓐ $43.22
Ⓑ $47.93
Ⓒ $51.78
Ⓓ $56.50

10. Sally bought milk for $2.80. Tax in her state is 7%. What was the total amount that Sally paid for the milk?
Ⓐ $2.60
Ⓑ $2.87
Ⓒ $3.00
Ⓓ $3.50

Exponents

Answer the questions below.

1. $5^4 =$
- (A) $5 + 5 + 5 + 5$
- (B) $5 \times 5 \times 5 \times 5$
- (C) $4 + 4 + 4 + 4 + 4$
- (D) $4 \times 4 \times 4 \times 4 \times 4$

2. $7 \times 7 \times 7 \times 7 \times 7 =$
- (A) 7^5
- (B) 5^7
- (C) 35
- (D) $\frac{7}{5}$

3. $8^4 =$
- (A) 32
- (B) 64
- (C) $4,096$
- (D) $65,536$

4. Four cubed is
- (A) $4 \times 4 \times 4 \times 4 \times 4 = 4^5 = 1,024$
- (B) $4 \times 4 \times 4 \times 4 = 4^4 = 256$
- (C) $4 \times 4 \times 4 = 4^3 = 64$
- (D) $4 \times 4 = 4^2 = 16$

5. $10^6 =$
- (A) $10,000$
- (B) $100,000$
- (C) $1,000,000$
- (D) $10,000,000$

6. What is the sixth power of 2?
- (A) $6^2 = 12$
- (B) $2^6 = 64$
- (C) $6^2 = 36$
- (D) $2^6 = 12$

7. $(1 \times 10^6) + (7 \times 10^4) + (4 \times 10^3) + (2 \times 10^0) =$
- (A) $1,742$
- (B) $10,742$
- (C) $1,074,002$
- (D) $100,742$

8. $(1 \times 10^5) + (2 \times 10^2) + (4 \times 10^3) =$
- (A) $10,420$
- (B) $104,200$
- (C) $244,200$
- (D) $284,000$

9. $15,934 =$
- (A) $(1 \times 10^5) + (5 \times 10^4) + (9 \times 10^3) + (3 \times 10^2) + (4 \times 10^0)$
- (B) $(1 \times 10^6) + (5 \times 10^4) + (9 \times 10^3) + (3 \times 10^2) + (4 \times 10^0)$
- (C) $(1 \times 10^5) + (5 \times 10^4) + (9 \times 10^3) + (3 \times 10^2) + (4 \times 10^1)$
- (D) $(1 \times 10^4) + (5 \times 10^3) + (9 \times 10^2) + (3 \times 10^1) + (4 \times 10^0)$

10. $15,625 =$
- (A) $(1 \times 10^4) + (5 \times 10^4) + (6 \times 10^3) + (2 \times 10^2) + (5 \times 10^1)$
- (B) $(1 \times 10^4) + (5 \times 10^4) + (6 \times 10^3) + (2 \times 10^1) + (5 \times 10^1)$
- (C) $(1 \times 10^5) + (5 \times 10^3) + (6 \times 10^3) + (2 \times 10^1) + (5 \times 10^0)$
- (D) $(1 \times 10^4) + (5 \times 10^3) + (6 \times 10^2) + (2 \times 10^1) + (5 \times 10^0)$

Positive and Negative Integers

Answer the questions below.

1. −3 + 1 =
  Ⓐ 4
  Ⓑ −2
  Ⓒ 2
  Ⓓ −4

2. −1 − (−7) =
  Ⓐ 6
  Ⓑ −8
  Ⓒ 8
  Ⓓ −6

3. −8 + −6 =
  Ⓐ 14
  Ⓑ −14
  Ⓒ 2
  Ⓓ −2

4. 3 − (−8) =
  Ⓐ 5
  Ⓑ −5
  Ⓒ −11
  Ⓓ 11

5. 6 + (−2) =
  Ⓐ 8
  Ⓑ 4
  Ⓒ −8
  Ⓓ −4

6. −7 − (−9) =
  Ⓐ −16
  Ⓑ −2
  Ⓒ 16
  Ⓓ 2

7. −9 + (−2) =
  Ⓐ −11
  Ⓑ 7
  Ⓒ 11
  Ⓓ −7

8. 0 − (−13) =
  Ⓐ 3
  Ⓑ 0
  Ⓒ 13
  Ⓓ −13

9. −4 + 3 =
  Ⓐ 7
  Ⓑ −7
  Ⓒ 1
  Ⓓ −1

10. −11 − (−14) =
  Ⓐ 3
  Ⓑ −3
  Ⓒ 25
  Ⓓ −25

11. 17 + (−6) =
  Ⓐ −11
  Ⓑ 11
  Ⓒ 23
  Ⓓ −23

12. −36 − 29 =
  Ⓐ −65
  Ⓑ 65
  Ⓒ 7
  Ⓓ −7

Section 5: Algebra and Functions
Number Patterns

Answer the questions below.

1. Which number completes this pattern:
2, 4, __, 8, 10?
- Ⓐ 3
- Ⓑ 5
- Ⓒ 6
- Ⓓ 7

2. Which number comes next in this pattern:
3, 7, 11, 15, __?
- Ⓐ 16
- Ⓑ 17
- Ⓒ 18
- Ⓓ 19

3. Which number completes this pattern:
4, 8, 16, __, 64?
- Ⓐ 22
- Ⓑ 28
- Ⓒ 32
- Ⓓ 34

4. Which number completes this pattern:
5, 7, __, 11, 13?
- Ⓐ 9
- Ⓑ 8
- Ⓒ 7
- Ⓓ 6

5. Which number comes next in this pattern:
80, 40, 20, 10, __?
- Ⓐ 30
- Ⓑ 5
- Ⓒ 0
- Ⓓ 15

6. Which number completes this pattern:
31, 28, 25, __, 19, 16?
- Ⓐ 22
- Ⓑ 24
- Ⓒ 23
- Ⓓ 21

7. What is the rule for this number pattern:
100, 83, 66, 49, 32, 15?
- Ⓐ subtract 7
- Ⓑ divide by 3
- Ⓒ subtract 17
- Ⓓ divide by 5

8. What is the rule for this number pattern:
270, 90, 30, 10?
- Ⓐ subtract 180
- Ⓑ divide by 9
- Ⓒ add 180
- Ⓓ divide by 3

9. What is the rule for this number pattern:
5, 20, 80, 320?
- Ⓐ multiply by 4
- Ⓑ add 4
- Ⓒ subtract 4
- Ⓓ divide by 4

10. What is the rule for this number pattern:
2, 6, 18, 54, 162?
- Ⓐ add 4
- Ⓑ multiply by 3
- Ⓒ multiply by 4
- Ⓓ add 12

11. What is the rule for this number pattern:
27, 35, 43, 51, 59?
- Ⓐ add 9
- Ⓑ multiply by 2
- Ⓒ add 8
- Ⓓ multiply by 3

12. What is the rule for this number pattern:
160, 40, 10?
- Ⓐ divide by 4
- Ⓑ multiply by 4
- Ⓒ add 4
- Ⓓ subtract 4

Algebraic and Numerical Expressions

Choose the expression that best represents the word problem.

1. Jill had seven rabbits, but gave some away.
- (A) $7 - x$
- (B) $7 \mid x$
- (C) $x - 7$
- (D) $x + 7$

2. Samuel ate three carrots, then he ate some more.
- (A) $3 - t$
- (B) $3 + t$
- (C) $t - 3$
- (D) $3 \div t$

3. Sara had nine nickels. She dropped some, then found two more.
- (A) $z - 9 + 2$
- (B) $2 - z + 9$
- (C) $9 + z - 2$
- (D) $9 - z + 2$

4. Craig had some baseball cards, then he sold four of them.
- (A) $d + 4$
- (B) $d - 4$
- (C) $4 - d$
- (D) $4 + d$

5. Cindy read some books, then she read twelve more.
- (A) $r \times 12$
- (B) $r - 12$
- (C) $r + 12$
- (D) $r \div 12$

6. Jack baked some cookies. He made four more, then ate two.
- (A) $q + 4 - 2$
- (B) $2 - q + 4$
- (C) $q - 2 + 4$
- (D) $4 - q + 2$

Evaluate the expression.

7. $x + 7$, when $x = 4$
- (A) 9
- (B) 10
- (C) 11
- (D) 12

8. $13 - y$, when $y = 8$
- (A) 4
- (B) 5
- (C) 6
- (D) 7

9. $22 - s$, when $s = 6$
- (A) 13
- (B) 14
- (C) 15
- (D) 16

10. $15 + g$, when $g = 11$
- (A) 23
- (B) 24
- (C) 25
- (D) 26

11. $j - 4$, when $j = 9$
- (A) 5
- (B) 6
- (C) 7
- (D) 8

12. $e \times 6$, when $e = 7$
- (A) 42
- (B) 43
- (C) 44
- (D) 45

Adding and Subtracting Equations

Solve for the variable.

1. $4 + x = 7$
- Ⓐ 2
- Ⓑ 3
- Ⓒ 4
- Ⓓ 11

2. $t - 8 = 3$
- Ⓐ 11
- Ⓑ 10
- Ⓒ 9
- Ⓓ 8

3. $m + 13 = 19$
- Ⓐ 32
- Ⓑ 22
- Ⓒ 8
- Ⓓ 6

4. $23 - z = 14$
- Ⓐ 8
- Ⓑ 9
- Ⓒ 27
- Ⓓ 37

5. $39 + h = 57$
- Ⓐ 18
- Ⓑ 28
- Ⓒ 86
- Ⓓ 96

6. $32 - 18 = k$
- Ⓐ 12
- Ⓑ 13
- Ⓒ 14
- Ⓓ 15

7. $102 - d = 47$
- Ⓐ 149
- Ⓑ 75
- Ⓒ 45
- Ⓓ 55

8. $68 = q + 43$
- Ⓐ 15
- Ⓑ 25
- Ⓒ 101
- Ⓓ 111

9. $j + 85 = 100$
- Ⓐ 15
- Ⓑ 21
- Ⓒ 13
- Ⓓ 19

10. $96 = a + 29$
- Ⓐ 65
- Ⓑ 67
- Ⓒ 73
- Ⓓ 51

11. $116 + y = 144$
- Ⓐ 25
- Ⓑ 38
- Ⓒ 32
- Ⓓ 28

12. $f - 8 = 72$
- Ⓐ 90
- Ⓑ 85
- Ⓒ 80
- Ⓓ 88

13. Janet's soccer team won the game with seven points. If three points were scored in the first half, how many points were scored in the second half?
- Ⓐ 2
- Ⓑ 3
- Ⓒ 4
- Ⓓ 5

14. Marc had eighteen pieces of candy. He gave some candy to his friends and was left with seven pieces. How many pieces of candy did he give to his friends?
- Ⓐ 7
- Ⓑ 11
- Ⓒ 21
- Ⓓ 25

Multiplying and Dividing Equations

Solve for the variable.

1. $3 \times f = 15$
- (A) 3
- (B) 4
- (C) 5
- (D) 6

2. $42 \div e = 7$
- (A) 6
- (B) 7
- (C) 8
- (D) 9

3. $36 = 6 \times v$
- (A) 5
- (B) 6
- (C) 7
- (D) 8

4. $75 \div a = 5$
- (A) 12
- (B) 13
- (C) 14
- (D) 15

5. $104 = j \times 4$
- (A) 27
- (B) 26
- (C) 25
- (D) 24

6. $x \div 13 = 7$
- (A) 84
- (B) 87
- (C) 91
- (D) 93

7. $b \times 57 = 627$
- (A) 12
- (B) 11
- (C) 10
- (D) 9

8. $243 \div l = 3$
- (A) 79
- (B) 80
- (C) 81
- (D) 82

9. $55 \div c = 11$
- (A) 3
- (B) 4
- (C) 5
- (D) 6

10. $g \times 6 = 72$
- (A) 15
- (B) 14
- (C) 13
- (D) 12

11. $99 = m \times 9$
- (A) 11
- (B) 21
- (C) 18
- (D) 9

12. $t \div 5 = 45$
- (A) 250
- (B) 225
- (C) 200
- (D) 25

13. Joanne eats three meals a day. If she has eaten twelve meals this week, then how many days has it been?
- (A) 6
- (B) 5
- (C) 4
- (D) 3

14. Jimmy has 32 pieces of paper. He splits them into stacks of 8 sheets. How many stacks does he have?
- (A) 3
- (B) 4
- (C) 5
- (D) 6

Inequalities

Answer the questions below.

1. Which number is a
solution to $x + 3 > 9$?
Ⓐ 5
Ⓑ 4
Ⓒ 7
Ⓓ 6

2. Which number is a
solution to $6 - x < 3$?
Ⓐ 4
Ⓑ 1
Ⓒ 3
Ⓓ 2

3. Which number is a
solution to $x + 5 < 7$?
Ⓐ 2
Ⓑ 1
Ⓒ 3
Ⓓ 4

4. Which number is a
solution to $x - 4 > 3$?
Ⓐ 6
Ⓑ 5
Ⓒ 4
Ⓓ 7

5. Which number is a
solution to $x + 2 \geqslant 6$?
Ⓐ 2
Ⓑ 3
Ⓒ 4
Ⓓ 1

6. Which number is a
solution to $7 - x \leqslant 3$?
Ⓐ 1
Ⓑ 4
Ⓒ 3
Ⓓ 2

7. Which number is **not** a
solution to $x - 4 > 1$?
Ⓐ 7
Ⓑ 4
Ⓒ 8
Ⓓ 6

8. Which number is **not** a
solution to $3 + x > 9$?
Ⓐ 6
Ⓑ 8
Ⓒ 7
Ⓓ 9

9. Which number is **not** a
solution to $x + 1 \geqslant 5$?
Ⓐ 5
Ⓑ 4
Ⓒ 6
Ⓓ 3

10. Which number is **not** a
solution to $x - 1 < 3$?
Ⓐ 2
Ⓑ 4
Ⓒ 1
Ⓓ 3

11. Which number is **not** a
solution to $2 + x < 5$?
Ⓐ 2
Ⓑ 0
Ⓒ 3
Ⓓ 1

12. Which number is **not** a
solution to $x - 3 \leqslant 7$?
Ⓐ 10
Ⓑ 8
Ⓒ 9
Ⓓ 11

Graphing Ordered Pairs

Use the following graph to answer questions 1–4.

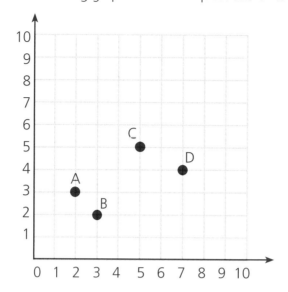

1. Which ordered pair represents point A?
- Ⓐ (3,2)
- Ⓑ (2,3)
- Ⓒ (5,5)
- Ⓓ (4,7)

2. Which ordered pair represents point C?
- Ⓐ (7,4)
- Ⓑ (4,7)
- Ⓒ (2,3)
- Ⓓ (5,5)

3. Which ordered pair represents point D?
- Ⓐ (4,7)
- Ⓑ (2,3)
- Ⓒ (7,4)
- Ⓓ (3,2)

4. Which ordered pair represents point B?
- Ⓐ (3,2)
- Ⓑ (2,3)
- Ⓒ (5,5)
- Ⓓ (7,4)

Use the following graph to answer questions 5–8.

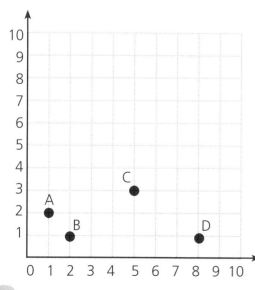

5. Which point is (5,3)?
- Ⓐ A
- Ⓑ B
- Ⓒ C
- Ⓓ D

6. Which point is (2,1)?
- Ⓐ A
- Ⓑ B
- Ⓒ C
- Ⓓ D

7. Which point is (8,1)?
- Ⓐ A
- Ⓑ B
- Ⓒ C
- Ⓓ D

8. Which point is (1,2)?
- Ⓐ A
- Ⓑ B
- Ⓒ C
- Ⓓ D

Linear Functions

Answer the questions below.

1. Which function represents the following data set?

x	y
1	5
2	6
3	7

- Ⓐ $y = x + 4$
- Ⓑ $x = y + 4$
- Ⓒ $y = 5x$
- Ⓓ $x = 5y$

2. Which of the data sets would be given by the function $y = 4x$?

Ⓐ
x	y
−1	0
0	0
1	0

Ⓑ
x	y
−1	−4
0	−3
1	−2

Ⓒ
x	y
−1	2
0	3
1	4

Ⓓ
x	y
−1	−4
0	0
1	4

3. Which of the data sets would be given by the function $y = 9 - 2x$?

Ⓐ
x	y
−1	11
0	12
1	13

Ⓑ
x	y
−1	11
0	9
1	7

Ⓒ
x	y
−1	7
0	9
1	11

Ⓓ
x	y
−1	1
0	4
1	7

4. Which function represents the following data set?

x	y
3	3
5	1
7	−1

- Ⓐ $-y = x + 6$
- Ⓑ $x = -6y$
- Ⓒ $y = -x + 6$
- Ⓓ $y = -6x$

Evaluate the functions for y.

5. $y = 7x - 4$, when $x = 3$
- Ⓐ 1
- Ⓑ 13
- Ⓒ −7
- Ⓓ 17

6. $x = 2y + 3$, when $x = 1$
- Ⓐ −1
- Ⓑ 0
- Ⓒ 1
- Ⓓ 5

7. $y = 8x$, when $x = 5$
- Ⓐ 0
- Ⓑ $\frac{5}{8}$
- Ⓒ 40
- Ⓓ 50

8. $y = -(2x + 4)$, when $x = 0$
- Ⓐ 0
- Ⓑ −4
- Ⓒ 4
- Ⓓ 2

Section 6: Measurement and Geometry

Lines, Angles, and Polygons

Use the graph below to answer questions 1–4.

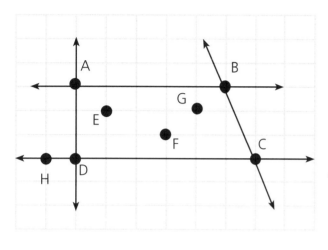

1. Which angle is a right angle?
- Ⓐ ∠ADC
- Ⓑ ∠HDC
- Ⓒ ∠ABC
- Ⓓ ∠BCD

2. Which angle is an obtuse angle?
- Ⓐ ∠ADC
- Ⓑ ∠HDC
- Ⓒ ∠ABC
- Ⓓ ∠BCD

3. Which angle is an acute angle?
- Ⓐ ∠ADC
- Ⓑ ∠HDC
- Ⓒ ∠ABC
- Ⓓ ∠BCD

4. Which angle is a straight angle?
- Ⓐ ∠ADC
- Ⓑ ∠HDC
- Ⓒ ∠ABC
- Ⓓ ∠BCD

Use the graph below to answer questions 5–8.

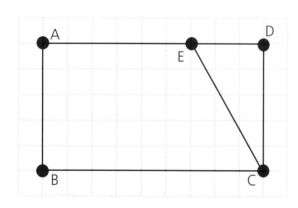

5. Which line segments are perpendicular to $\overline{AB}$?
- Ⓐ $\overline{EC}$ and $\overline{CD}$
- Ⓑ $\overline{ED}$ and $\overline{EC}$
- Ⓒ $\overline{AD}$ and $\overline{BC}$
- Ⓓ $\overline{BC}$ and $\overline{DC}$

6. Which line segment is parallel to $\overline{CD}$?
- Ⓐ $\overline{AB}$
- Ⓑ $\overline{AD}$
- Ⓒ $\overline{BC}$
- Ⓓ $\overline{EC}$

7. Which line segments are perpendicular to $\overline{BC}$?
- Ⓐ $\overline{EC}$ and $\overline{CD}$
- Ⓑ $\overline{AD}$ and $\overline{DE}$
- Ⓒ $\overline{AB}$ and $\overline{AE}$
- Ⓓ $\overline{AB}$ and $\overline{CD}$

8. Which line segment is parallel to $\overline{DE}$?
- Ⓐ $\overline{BC}$
- Ⓑ $\overline{CE}$
- Ⓒ $\overline{AB}$
- Ⓓ $\overline{CD}$

Triangles and Quadrilaterals

Identify the type of triangle.

1.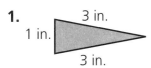
3 in.
1 in.
3 in.
- Ⓐ equilateral
- Ⓑ isosceles
- Ⓒ scalene
- Ⓓ obtuse

2.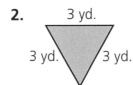
3 yd.
3 yd. 3 yd.
- Ⓐ equilateral
- Ⓑ isosceles
- Ⓒ scalene
- Ⓓ right

3.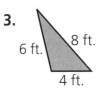
8 ft.
6 ft.
4 ft.
- Ⓐ equilateral
- Ⓑ isosceles
- Ⓒ scalene
- Ⓓ acute

4.
- Ⓐ acute
- Ⓑ obtuse
- Ⓒ right
- Ⓓ scalene

5.
- Ⓐ acute
- Ⓑ obtuse
- Ⓒ right
- Ⓓ equilateral

6.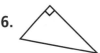
- Ⓐ acute
- Ⓑ obtuse
- Ⓒ right
- Ⓓ isosceles

Identify the type of quadrilateral.

7.
- Ⓐ rhombus
- Ⓑ trapezoid
- Ⓒ square
- Ⓓ parallelogram

8.
- Ⓐ trapezoid
- Ⓑ rhombus
- Ⓒ square
- Ⓓ rectangle

9.
- Ⓐ triangle
- Ⓑ rectangle
- Ⓒ trapezoid
- Ⓓ rhombus

10.
- Ⓐ rectangle
- Ⓑ trapezoid
- Ⓒ triangle
- Ⓓ parallelogram

Congruent and Similar Figures

Determine the type of relationship of the shapes in each problem.

1.

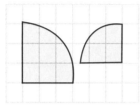

Ⓐ congruent
Ⓑ similar
Ⓒ congruent and similar
Ⓓ neither

2.

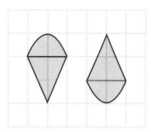

Ⓐ congruent
Ⓑ similar
Ⓒ congruent and similar
Ⓓ neither

3.

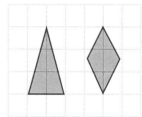

Ⓐ congruent
Ⓑ similar
Ⓒ congruent and similar
Ⓓ neither

4.

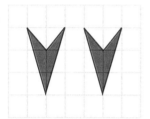

Ⓐ congruent
Ⓑ similar
Ⓒ congruent and similar
Ⓓ neither

5.

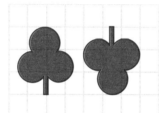

Ⓐ congruent
Ⓑ similar
Ⓒ congruent and similar
Ⓓ neither

6.

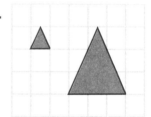

Ⓐ congruent
Ⓑ similar
Ⓒ congruent and similar
Ⓓ neither

Use the following shapes to answer questions 7–9.

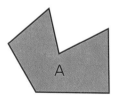 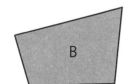  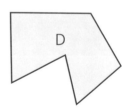 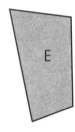

7. Which two shapes are similar?
Ⓐ A and B
Ⓑ B and D
Ⓒ A and D
Ⓓ C and D

8. Which two shapes are congruent?
Ⓐ B and E
Ⓑ A and D
Ⓒ B and C
Ⓓ C and D

9. Which two shapes are similar but **not** congruent?
Ⓐ B and E
Ⓑ A and D
Ⓒ C and D
Ⓓ B and D

Perimeter

Find the perimeter of each polygon.

1.

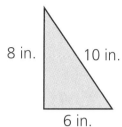

8 in. 10 in.

6 in.

- Ⓐ 14 in.
- Ⓑ 18 in.
- Ⓒ 22 in.
- Ⓓ 24 in.

2.

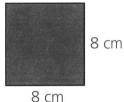

8 cm

8 cm

- Ⓐ 8 cm
- Ⓑ 16 cm
- Ⓒ 32 cm
- Ⓓ 64 cm

3.

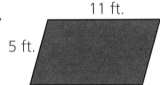

11 ft.

5 ft.

- Ⓐ 16 ft.
- Ⓑ 32 ft.
- Ⓒ 43 ft.
- Ⓓ 55 ft.

4.

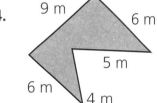

9 m 6 m

5 m

6 m 4 m

- Ⓐ 30 m
- Ⓑ 27 m
- Ⓒ 25 m
- Ⓓ 20 m

Answer the questions.

5. Magdalena wants to make a rectangular garden that has a perimeter of 36 feet. If the length will be 10 feet, what should the width be?
- Ⓐ 6 feet
- Ⓑ 8 feet
- Ⓒ 10 feet
- Ⓓ 12 feet

6. Gene needs a piece of paper that has a length of 10 inches and a width of 12 inches. What is the perimeter of his paper?
- Ⓐ 12 inches
- Ⓑ 22 inches
- Ⓒ 32 inches
- Ⓓ 44 inches

7. June wants a tree fort that is 4 feet wide and 3 feet long. What is the perimeter of her tree fort?
- Ⓐ 7 feet
- Ⓑ 12 feet
- Ⓒ 14 feet
- Ⓓ 16 feet

8. The school's new football field is 100 yards long and has a perimeter of 308 yards. What is the width of the field?
- Ⓐ 208 yards
- Ⓑ 108 yards
- Ⓒ 64 yards
- Ⓓ 54 yards

Area

Find the area of each polygon.

1.

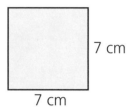

7 cm

7 cm

(A) 14 cm²
(B) 28 cm²
(C) 42 cm²
(D) 49 cm²

2.

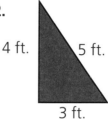

4 ft.   5 ft.

3 ft.

(A) 24 ft.²
(B) 12 ft.²
(C) 6 ft.²
(D) 3 ft.²

3.

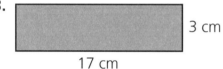

3 cm

17 cm

(A) 51 m²
(B) 41 m²
(C) 40 m²
(D) 20 m²

4.

11 in.

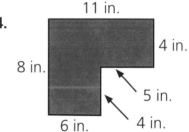

4 in.

8 in.

5 in.

6 in.   4 in.

(A) 88 in.²
(B) 68 in.²
(C) 38 in.²
(D) 19 in.²

Use the following shapes to help you answer questions 5–8.

Area = 24

Area = 10.5

Area = 81

Area = 10

5. Which formula is used to find the area of a rectangle?
(A) length + width
(B) length × length
(C) (length × 2) + (width × 2)
(D) length × width

6. Which formula is used to find the area of a triangle?
(A) $\frac{1}{2}$ base × height
(B) base × height
(C) $\frac{1}{2}$ base × $\frac{1}{2}$ height
(D) base + height

7. Which formula is used to find the area of a square?
(A) $\frac{1}{2}$ length × $\frac{1}{2}$ length
(B) length × length
(C) length + length
(D) 4 × length

8. Which formula is used to find the area of a parallelogram?
(A) (length × 2) + (width × 2)
(B) length + width
(C) length × width
(D) $\frac{1}{2}$ length × $\frac{1}{2}$ width

Volume

Find the volume of each rectangular prism.

1. Adrienne was curious how much space her fridge took up. She found out that it was 4 feet high, 2 feet wide, and 3 feet long. What is the volume of her fridge?

Ⓐ 6 ft.³
Ⓑ 8 ft.³
Ⓒ 12 ft.³
Ⓓ 24 ft.³

2.

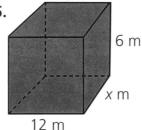

8 m
4 m
5 m

Ⓐ 40 m³
Ⓑ 80 m³
Ⓒ 160 m³
Ⓓ 320 m³

3.

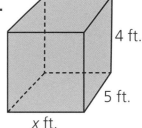

7 yd.
5 yd.
6 yd.

Ⓐ 210 yd.³
Ⓑ 105 yd.³
Ⓒ 42 yd.³
Ⓓ 35 yd.³

Find the missing measurement.

4.

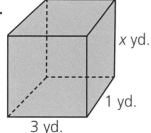

x yd.
1 yd.
3 yd.
Volume = 6 yd.³

Ⓐ 1 yd.
Ⓑ 2 yd.
Ⓒ 3 yd.
Ⓓ 6 yd.

5.

6 m
x m
12 m
Volume = 360 m³

Ⓐ 4 m
Ⓑ 5 m
Ⓒ 6 m
Ⓓ 12 m

6.

4 ft.
5 ft.
x ft.
Volume = 160 ft.³

Ⓐ 4 ft.
Ⓑ 5 ft.
Ⓒ 6 ft.
Ⓓ 8 ft.

Answer the questions.

7. A cardboard box has a length of 3 feet, a width of 3 feet, and a height of 2 feet. If the box is filled halfway with packing peanuts, what is the volume of the peanuts?

Ⓐ 6 ft.³
Ⓑ 8 ft.³
Ⓒ 9 ft.³
Ⓓ 18 ft.³

8. A rectangular hole is dug with a volume of 30 m³. If 5 m³ of rocks is poured into the hole, how much empty space is left?

Ⓐ 25 m³
Ⓑ 15 m³
Ⓒ 6 m³
Ⓓ 5 m³

Working with Measurements

Answer the questions below.

1. Which unit would be **best** used to measure the height of a house?
   Ⓐ feet
   Ⓑ inches
   Ⓒ miles
   Ⓓ ounces

2. Which of these is the least amount of liquid?
   Ⓐ 1 gallon
   Ⓑ 3 pints
   Ⓒ 2 quarts
   Ⓓ 4 cups

3. How many feet are equal to 23 yards?
   Ⓐ 46 feet
   Ⓑ 69 feet
   Ⓒ 82 feet
   Ⓓ 92 feet

4. Which measurement is equal to 2 meters?
   Ⓐ 2,000 centimeters
   Ⓑ 0.02 kilometers
   Ⓒ 20 centimeters
   Ⓓ 2,000 millimeters

5. Which measurement of length is the largest?
   Ⓐ 5,000 feet
   Ⓑ 1 mile
   Ⓒ 900 yards
   Ⓓ 1 kilometer

6. Which unit would be **best** used to measure the height of a mountain?
   Ⓐ feet
   Ⓑ inches
   Ⓒ miles
   Ⓓ yards

7. Which measurement is equal to 39 centimeters?
   Ⓐ 2 feet
   Ⓑ 25 inches
   Ⓒ 390 meter
   Ⓓ 390 millimeters

8. How many inches are equal to 110 feet?
   Ⓐ 132
   Ⓑ 220
   Ⓒ 1,320
   Ⓓ 1,420

9. Which unit would be **best** used to measure the weight of a small feather?
   - Ⓐ pounds
   - Ⓑ ounces
   - Ⓒ grams
   - Ⓓ tons

10. Which amount is equal to 0.5 gallons?
    - Ⓐ 3 quarts
    - Ⓑ 2 pints
    - Ⓒ 64 ounces
    - Ⓓ 6 cups

11. Which unit would be **best** used to measure the amount of water in a swimming pool?
    - Ⓐ cups
    - Ⓑ gallons
    - Ⓒ liters
    - Ⓓ pints

12. Kelly is making a cake. The recipe calls for 1 cup of water. Kelly's measuring cup only measures in ounces. How many ounces does she need?
    - Ⓐ 4
    - Ⓑ 6
    - Ⓒ 8
    - Ⓓ 10

13. Which answer has the units of measurement in order from lightest to heaviest?
    - Ⓐ gram, ounce, pound, ton
    - Ⓑ ton, pound, ounce, gram
    - Ⓒ gram, pound, ounce, ton
    - Ⓓ ounce, gram, pound, ton

14. Which amount is equal to 64 ounces?
    - Ⓐ 2 quarts
    - Ⓑ 1 gallon
    - Ⓒ 3 liters
    - Ⓓ 2 pints

15. How many pounds are in a ton?
    - Ⓐ 1,200 pounds
    - Ⓑ 1,800 pounds
    - Ⓒ 2,000 pounds
    - Ⓓ 3,000 pounds

16. Which unit would be **best** used to measure the distance between two cities?
    - Ⓐ centimeters
    - Ⓑ inches
    - Ⓒ feet
    - Ⓓ miles

Transformations

Use the shapes below to answer questions 1–6.

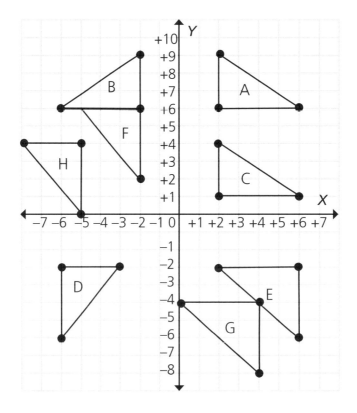

1. Which figure could result from a translation of Triangle A?
   - Ⓐ Triangle B
   - Ⓑ Triangle C
   - Ⓒ Triangle D
   - Ⓓ Triangle E

2. Which figure could result from a rotation of Triangle B?
   - Ⓐ Triangle F
   - Ⓑ Triangle E
   - Ⓒ Triangle D
   - Ⓓ Triangle C

3. Which figure could result from a reflection of Triangle A?
   - Ⓐ Triangle D
   - Ⓑ Triangle C
   - Ⓒ Triangle B
   - Ⓓ Triangle E

4. Which figure could result from a translation of Triangle H?
   - Ⓐ Triangle C
   - Ⓑ Triangle B
   - Ⓒ Triangle F
   - Ⓓ Triangle G

5. Which shape is the same as Triangle C rotated 90° clockwise and then translated?
   - Ⓐ Triangle G
   - Ⓑ Triangle F
   - Ⓒ Triangle E
   - Ⓓ Triangle D

6. What would you do to Triangle E to get Triangle G?
   - Ⓐ reflection
   - Ⓑ 45° rotation
   - Ⓒ translation
   - Ⓓ 90° rotation

Section 7: Statistics, Data Analysis, and Probability

Working with Probability

Answer the questions below. Reduce all fractions to the simplest form.

1. If there are 13 clubs in a deck of 52 cards, then what is the probability that a card drawn at random will be a club?

ⓐ $\frac{1}{4}$

ⓑ $\frac{1}{8}$

ⓒ $\frac{13}{52}$

ⓓ $\frac{39}{52}$

2. Noah has a bag of 30 marbles. Of these marbles, 8 are blue, 9 are red, and the rest are clear. What is the probability that a marble taken from the bag will **not** be red?

ⓐ $\frac{3}{10}$

ⓑ $\frac{7}{10}$

ⓒ $\frac{17}{30}$

ⓓ $\frac{13}{30}$

3. Penelope grew 33 tomatoes in her garden. If $\frac{1}{3}$ of her tomatoes went bad, how many tomatoes are left?

ⓐ 11

ⓑ 15

ⓒ 22

ⓓ 27

4. Michael bought 10 boxes of cereal. If $\frac{1}{5}$ of the boxes have a prize in them, how many prizes did he get?

ⓐ 1

ⓑ 2

ⓒ 3

ⓓ 5

Use the picture below to answer questions 5–8. Reduce all fractions to the simplest form.

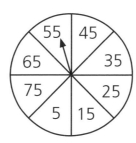

5. What is the probability of the spinner landing on a number less than 20?

ⓐ $\frac{1}{4}$

ⓑ $\frac{1}{8}$

ⓒ $\frac{2}{8}$

ⓓ $\frac{2}{6}$

6. What is the probability that the spinner will land on 45 or greater?

ⓐ $\frac{1}{4}$

ⓑ $\frac{1}{8}$

ⓒ $\frac{1}{2}$

ⓓ $\frac{5}{8}$

7. What is the probability that the spinner will land on a number that is **not** 65?

ⓐ $\frac{1}{8}$

ⓑ $\frac{1}{4}$

ⓒ $\frac{6}{7}$

ⓓ $\frac{7}{8}$

8. What is the probability that the spinner will land on a number less than 20 or a number more than 70?

ⓐ $\frac{1}{4}$

ⓑ $\frac{3}{8}$

ⓒ $\frac{3}{5}$

ⓓ $\frac{5}{8}$

Mean, Median, Mode, and Range

Solve the problems below.

1. What is the mean of 7, 3, 5, 6, 9?
- Ⓐ 5
- Ⓑ 6
- Ⓒ 7
- Ⓓ 8

2. What is the mean of 50, 30, 75, 45, 90, 70?
- Ⓐ 60
- Ⓑ 50
- Ⓒ 45
- Ⓓ 35

3. What is the mean of 130, 250, 90, 370?
- Ⓐ 300
- Ⓑ 110
- Ⓒ 170
- Ⓓ 210

4. What is the median of 9, 12, 3, 8, 6?
- Ⓐ 12
- Ⓑ 3
- Ⓒ 8
- Ⓓ 6

5. What is the median of 34, 60, 56, 15, 90, 40?
- Ⓐ 40
- Ⓑ 42
- Ⓒ 56
- Ⓓ 48

6. What is the median of 450, 280, 360, 100?
- Ⓐ 320
- Ⓑ 280
- Ⓒ 360
- Ⓓ 340

7. What is the mode of 1, 7, 3, 5, 9, 4, 5?
- Ⓐ 1
- Ⓑ 5
- Ⓒ 7
- Ⓓ no mode

8. What is the mode of 3, 9, 9, 6, 4, 3, 2, 5, 3?
- Ⓐ 9
- Ⓑ 6
- Ⓒ 3
- Ⓓ no mode

9. What is the mode of 11, 19, 15, 27, 17, 32?
- Ⓐ 15
- Ⓑ 17
- Ⓒ 11
- Ⓓ no mode

10. What is the range of 55, 20, 35, 70, 45?
- Ⓐ 45
- Ⓑ 55
- Ⓒ 50
- Ⓓ 70

11. What is the range of 7, 3, 1, 8, 5, 6, 5, 4?
- Ⓐ 7
- Ⓑ 5
- Ⓒ 4
- Ⓓ 6

12. What is the range of 160, 340, 270?
- Ⓐ 160
- Ⓑ 180
- Ⓒ 270
- Ⓓ 340

Data in Tables and Graphs

Use the graph below to answer questions 1–4.

Professions with Much Walking	
Police officer	👣👣👣👣👣👣👣👣👣
Mail carrier	👣👣👣👣👣👣
TV reporter	👣👣👣👣👣
Doctor	👣👣👣👣
Key: 👣 = 200 miles/year	

1. Which profession requires the least amount of walking in a year?
Ⓐ police officer
Ⓑ mail carrier
Ⓒ TV reporter
Ⓓ doctor

2. What does each footprint represent?
Ⓐ 1 person
Ⓑ 3 hours
Ⓒ 200 miles/year
Ⓓ 200 years

3. Which profession requires about 1,600 miles of walking per year?
Ⓐ police officer
Ⓑ mail carrier
Ⓒ TV reporter
Ⓓ doctor

4. If construction workers walk about 700 miles per year, how many footprints would you use to represent them?
Ⓐ 3
Ⓑ 3.5
Ⓒ 4
Ⓓ 700

Use the line graph below to answer questions 5–8.

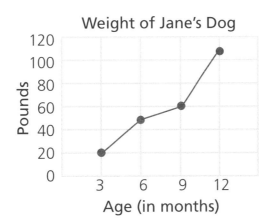

5. At about what age did Jane's dog weigh 60 pounds?
Ⓐ 3 months
Ⓑ 5 months
Ⓒ 7 months
Ⓓ 9 months

6. About how much did Jane's dog weigh when it was 6 months old?
Ⓐ 20 pounds
Ⓑ 45 pounds
Ⓒ 55 pounds
Ⓓ 60 pounds

7. When did Jane's dog weigh the most?
Ⓐ 3 months
Ⓑ 6 months
Ⓒ 9 months
Ⓓ 12 months

8. At about what age did Jane's dog weigh 80 pounds?
Ⓐ 8 months
Ⓑ 9 months
Ⓒ 10 months
Ⓓ 12 months

Section 8: Mathematical Reasoning
Problem-Solving Strategies
Solve the problems below.

1. Bonita bought several things at the clothing store. She spent $20 on jeans, $30 on shirts, $15 on earrings, and $35 on shoes. What type of graph would **best** represent how she spent her $100 dollars?
- Ⓐ line graph
- Ⓑ bar graph
- Ⓒ pie chart
- Ⓓ scatter plot

2. Jose is going to visit his sister, who lives 600 miles away. He has to switch trains when he is 200 miles from her house. What equation represents how far Jose is from home when he switches trains?
- Ⓐ $600 - 200 = x$
- Ⓑ $600 + 200 = x$
- Ⓒ $600 + x = 200$
- Ⓓ $x - 200 = 600$

3. Madison weighs less than Marc. Ming weighs less than Sam. Ming weighs more than Marc. Who weighs the most?
- Ⓐ Madison
- Ⓑ Marc
- Ⓒ Ming
- Ⓓ Sam

4. Jisela's birthday is 15 days before Cal's. Cal's birthday is 9 days after Henry's. Henry's birthday is on the 21st. Which expression represents when Jisela's birthday is?
- Ⓐ $21 + 9 + 15$
- Ⓑ $21 + 9 - 15$
- Ⓒ $21 - 9 + 15$
- Ⓓ $21 - 9 - 15$

5. Alex has three boxes of candy bars that he needs to sell. Each box weighs three pounds. The candy bars cost $2.00 each. Each bar weighs 0.25 pound. What information is **not** needed to determine the number of candy bars Alex has?
- Ⓐ cost of a candy bar
- Ⓑ weight of a box
- Ⓒ weight of a candy bar
- Ⓓ number of boxes

6. Aisha has eight boxes full of baseball cards. She needs only three more cards to complete her collection. What other information is needed to figure out how many cards are in the collection?
- Ⓐ the weight of a box
- Ⓑ the weight of a card
- Ⓒ the cost of a card
- Ⓓ the number of cards per box

7. Keira wants to add another room onto the back of her house. She has a small backyard with trees surrounding it. If she needs to measure the distance from the house to the trees, then what unit of measurement should she use?
Ⓐ inches
Ⓑ yards
Ⓒ miles
Ⓓ millimeters

8. What is the first step in solving for x in the equation $3x + 5 = 14$?
Ⓐ add 5 to both sides
Ⓑ divide both sides by 3
Ⓒ subtract 5 from both sides
Ⓓ multiply both sides by 3

9. Paolo had 15 video games. He let his friend borrow 3 and he rented 4 from the video store. What would be the **best** way to figure out how many video games Paolo has now?
Ⓐ make a list
Ⓑ find a pattern
Ⓒ make a table
Ⓓ write a number sentence

10. June needs to give each child the same amount of candy. What operation should she use to determine how much candy each child gets?
Ⓐ addition
Ⓑ subtraction
Ⓒ division
Ⓓ multiplication

11. Sarah wants to measure her living room to see if her new couch will fit. What is the **best** tool to help her?
Ⓐ scale
Ⓑ ruler
Ⓒ scissor
Ⓓ tape measure

12. Kris chews three pieces of gum per day. There are 10 pieces of gum in a pack. Which expression represents how many packs of gum Kris chews in a year?
Ⓐ $10 \times 3 + 365$
Ⓑ $3 \times 365 \div 10$
Ⓒ $10 \times 3 \times 365$
Ⓓ $365 \div 3 \times 10$

13. What is the first step in solving for x in the equation $3(x + 5) = 60$?
Ⓐ add 3 to both sides
Ⓑ subtract 5 from both sides
Ⓒ divide both sides by 3
Ⓓ multiply both sides by 3

14. Leah leaves the house at 8:30 AM and delivers 20 newspapers an hour. Each newspaper has a comics section. Her shift ends at 11:30 AM. What information is **not** needed to determine how many newpapers she delivers in all?
Ⓐ Each newspaper has a comics section.
Ⓑ Her shift ends at 11:30 AM.
Ⓒ She delivers 20 newspapers an hour.
Ⓓ She leaves the house at 8:30 AM.

Using Computation in Context

Read each problem carefully. Then solve the problems.

1. Natalie gets paid $5 to mow a lawn. If she makes $35 one day, how many lawns did she mow?
   - Ⓐ 5
   - Ⓑ 7
   - Ⓒ 3
   - Ⓓ 8

2. Geoffrey has two bags of marbles. One bag has 42 marbles and the other bag has 30 marbles. How many marbles would Geoffrey have to move so that he has the same number of marbles in each bag?
   - Ⓐ 6
   - Ⓑ 4
   - Ⓒ 8
   - Ⓓ 12

3. Jordan drove his car from Florida to Maine. He drove 2,359 miles total. What is the distance that Jordan drove, rounded to the nearest hundred?
   - Ⓐ 2,359 miles
   - Ⓑ 2,360 miles
   - Ⓒ 2,400 miles
   - Ⓓ 2,000 miles

4. The distance around the earth is about 25,000 miles. If a satellite travels around the earth x times, then which function represents the distance it has traveled?
   - Ⓐ $25,000y = x$
   - Ⓑ $\dfrac{x}{25,000} = y$
   - Ⓒ $25,000x = y$
   - Ⓓ $25,000 + x = y$

5. Benjamin Franklin was born in 1706. George Washington was born in 1732. How old was Franklin when Washington was born?
   - Ⓐ 16
   - Ⓑ 26
   - Ⓒ 36
   - Ⓓ 32

6. Mrs. Kendall's class plants 30 different kinds of flowers around the school. The class later figures out that 80% of the flowers bloomed. How many different kinds of flowers bloomed?
   - Ⓐ 2
   - Ⓑ 16
   - Ⓒ 28
   - Ⓓ 24

7. Turkey at the deli is $8.00 a pound. How much would it cost to buy 20 ounces of turkey?
Ⓐ $6.00
Ⓑ $8.50
Ⓒ $10.00
Ⓓ $16.00

8. A bus carrying ten people stops and picks up two more. At the next stop, four people get off. At the last stop, all but two people get off. How many people got off the bus at the last stop?
Ⓐ 4
Ⓑ 6
Ⓒ 8
Ⓓ 10

9. Water boils at 100°C. If it takes about 1.5 minutes for the water in a pot to go up one degree, how long will it take to boil water that is 88°C?
Ⓐ 18 minutes
Ⓑ 9 minutes
Ⓒ 13 minutes
Ⓓ 12.5 minutes

10. How far will a car traveling at 75 miles per hour travel in 100 minutes?
Ⓐ 7,500 miles
Ⓑ 125 miles
Ⓒ 1 hour 25 minutes
Ⓓ 125 minutes

11. Charlie hiked 6 miles on Tuesday, then double that amount on Thursday. If he hiked this many miles for 3 weeks, how many miles did he hike in all?
Ⓐ 58
Ⓑ 52
Ⓒ 54
Ⓓ 60

12. Aunt Suzie baked 6 dozen cookies for the bake sale. $\frac{1}{8}$ were chocolate chip. How many chocolate chip cookies did aunt Suzie bake?
Ⓐ 9
Ⓑ 8
Ⓒ 10
Ⓓ 11

13. Edward has 5 nickels, 10 dimes, and a quarter. He spends $1.25 on some candy at the fair. How much money does he have left over?
Ⓐ $1.90
Ⓑ $3.15
Ⓒ $1.50
Ⓓ $.25

14. Dulce buys a bag of 18 apples. She wants to keep half of the apples for herself and split the rest between 3 of her friends. How many apples will each of her friends get?
Ⓐ 2
Ⓑ 6
Ⓒ 9
Ⓓ 3

Section 9: Test

Solve the problems below.

1. What is the expanded form of 734,105?
- Ⓐ 700,000 + 30,000 + 4,000 + 100 + 50
- Ⓑ 700,000 + 30,000 + 4,000 + 100 + 5
- Ⓒ 700,000 + 34,000 + 105
- Ⓓ 70,000 + 3,000 + 400 + 10 + 5

2. 132,746
       + 78,534
- Ⓐ 211,270
- Ⓑ 54,212
- Ⓒ 210,280
- Ⓓ 211,280

3. 7^3 is the same as which of the following?
- Ⓐ 7 × 7 × 7
- Ⓑ 7 + 7 + 7
- Ⓒ 3 × 3 × 3 × 3 × 3 × 3 × 3
- Ⓓ 3 + 3 + 3 + 3 + 3 + 3 + 3

4. Kevin was curious how long it took him to get to school. He kept track of how long the bus ride was for a week. His times were 7 minutes, 8 minutes, 7.25 minutes, 8 minutes, and 7.75 minutes. What was the average time it took for Kevin to get to school?
- Ⓐ 8 minutes
- Ⓑ 7.9 minutes
- Ⓒ 7.6 minutes
- Ⓓ 7 minutes

5. Lindsay collects feathers. She has 15 seagull feathers, 7 crow feathers, 4 duck feathers, and 2 dove feathers. What is the probability that a feather taken from her collection at random will be a crow feather?
- Ⓐ $\frac{1}{4}$
- Ⓑ $\frac{1}{3}$
- Ⓒ $\frac{1}{28}$
- Ⓓ $\frac{7}{21}$

6. Which function would give the following data set?

x	y
1	5
2	8
3	11

- Ⓐ $x + 4 = y$
- Ⓑ $x - 4 = y$
- Ⓒ $3x + 2 = y$
- Ⓓ $2x + 3 = y$

7. Round 1,547.039 to the nearest hundredth.
- Ⓐ 1,547.039
- Ⓑ 1,547.04
- Ⓒ 1,500
- Ⓓ 2,000

8. Identify the shape.
- Ⓐ rhombus
- Ⓑ parallelogram
- Ⓒ triangle
- Ⓓ trapezoid

9. What is the formula for the area of a triangle?
- Ⓐ $\frac{1}{2}$ base × $\frac{1}{2}$ height
- Ⓑ base × height
- Ⓒ $\frac{1}{2}$ base × height
- Ⓓ base² × height

10. Which angle is an obtuse angle?
- Ⓐ 90°
- Ⓑ 103°
- Ⓒ 37°
- Ⓓ 73°

11. Evaluate $7x - 5 = y$ when $x = 4$.
- Ⓐ –7
- Ⓑ 30
- Ⓒ $1\frac{2}{7}$
- Ⓓ 23

12. What number completes this pattern:
17, 51, __, 459, 1, 377?
- Ⓐ 153
- Ⓑ 85
- Ⓒ 425
- Ⓓ 119

13. What is a solution to the inequality $3x - 2 \geqslant 3$?
- Ⓐ –1
- Ⓑ 0
- Ⓒ 1
- Ⓓ 2

14. What is 85% of 1,240?
- Ⓐ 105.4
- Ⓑ 1,458.8
- Ⓒ 1,054
- Ⓓ 145.9

15. Which property is demonstrated by the equation $3 + 5 = 5 + 3$?
- Ⓐ commutative
- Ⓑ associative
- Ⓒ distributive
- Ⓓ identity

16. If one of the angles in a right triangle is 36°, then how big is the other non-right angle?
- Ⓐ 234°
- Ⓑ 54°
- Ⓒ 99°
- Ⓓ 64°

17. Which fraction is equivalent to $\frac{3}{7}$?
- Ⓐ $\frac{12}{28}$
- Ⓑ $\frac{9}{20}$
- Ⓒ $\frac{12}{35}$
- Ⓓ $\frac{9}{22}$

18. Sue wants to buy seven pieces of candy. Each piece costs 75 cents. How much will her candy cost?
- Ⓐ $52.50
- Ⓑ $4.50
- Ⓒ $45.00
- Ⓓ $5.25

19. $3 - (-4) =$
- Ⓐ –1
- Ⓑ 7
- Ⓒ 1
- Ⓓ –7

20. What is the value of the underlined digit in 3.04<u>1</u>?
- Ⓐ $\frac{1}{100}$
- Ⓑ $\frac{1}{10}$
- Ⓒ $\frac{1}{1,000}$
- Ⓓ $\frac{1}{10,000}$

21. $\frac{3}{5} + \frac{2}{7} =$
- Ⓐ $\frac{31}{35}$
- Ⓑ $\frac{5}{12}$
- Ⓒ $\frac{25}{35}$
- Ⓓ $\frac{31}{70}$

22. Judy has a poster that is 24 inches wide and 16 inches long. What is the perimeter of the poster?
Ⓐ 42 inches
Ⓑ 80 inches
Ⓒ 216 inches
Ⓓ 432 inches

23. What is the greatest common factor of 24 and 18?
Ⓐ 4
Ⓑ 6
Ⓒ 8
Ⓓ 9

24. $1\frac{3}{7} \div \frac{4}{9} =$
Ⓐ $\frac{14}{45}$
Ⓑ $\frac{40}{63}$
Ⓒ $1\frac{23}{40}$
Ⓓ $3\frac{3}{14}$

25. What is the area of the rectangle shown below?

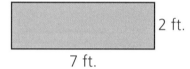

7 ft.

Ⓐ 18 ft.²
Ⓑ 16 ft.²
Ⓒ 14 ft.²
Ⓓ 9 ft.²

26. .047 × .372 =
Ⓐ .17
Ⓑ .017
Ⓒ .0017
Ⓓ .00017

27. What type of relationship do the following shapes have ?

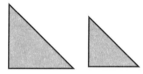

Ⓐ congruent
Ⓑ similar
Ⓒ congruent and similar
Ⓓ neither

28. What is the range of 19, 7, 24, 13, 9, 11?
Ⓐ 17
Ⓑ 12
Ⓒ 8
Ⓓ 7

29. William is faster than Heather. Andrea is slower than Carl. Andrea is faster than Heather. Who is the slowest?
Ⓐ William
Ⓑ Andrea
Ⓒ Heather
Ⓓ Carl

30. Which point on the graph below is at (3,5)?

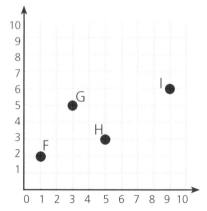

Ⓐ Point F
Ⓑ Point G
Ⓒ Point H
Ⓓ Point I

31. What type of triangle is the triangle below?

Ⓐ equilateral
Ⓑ isosceles
Ⓒ scalene
Ⓓ obtuse

32. Which number is 42 divisible by?

Ⓐ 3
Ⓑ 4
Ⓒ 5
Ⓓ 8

33. Which number makes $\frac{x}{32} = \frac{3}{4}$ a true statement?

Ⓐ 31
Ⓑ 21
Ⓒ 24
Ⓓ 27

34. $-13 - (-4) =$

Ⓐ -9
Ⓑ 9
Ⓒ -17
Ⓓ 17

35. Which equation **best** represents the statement: Stephanie had 13 apples, and then she sold some of them?

Ⓐ $35 + x$
Ⓑ $x - 13$
Ⓒ $x + 13$
Ⓓ $13 - x$

36. What is the height of the rectangular prism shown below?

Ⓐ 3 cm
Ⓑ 4 cm
Ⓒ 5 cm
Ⓓ 7 cm

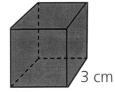

3 cm
7 cm
Volume = 105 cm³

37. $13\overline{)3{,}263}$

Ⓐ 251
Ⓑ 351
Ⓒ 237
Ⓓ 337

38. Round 375,213 to the nearest ten thousand.

Ⓐ 400,000
Ⓑ 380,000
Ⓒ 375,000
Ⓓ 370,000

39. $3^5 + 2^3 =$

Ⓐ 134
Ⓑ 251
Ⓒ 2,048,383
Ⓓ 14,706,125

40. Which data set would come from the function $y = 6x - 7$?

Ⓐ
x	y
2	5
4	17
6	31

Ⓑ
x	y
3	5
5	17
7	29

Ⓒ
x	y
2	11
4	23
6	35

Ⓓ
x	y
3	11
5	23
7	35

Answer Key

Pages 8–9
1. A
2. D
3. B
4. C
5. D
6. D
7. C
8. B
9. A
10. B

Pages 10–11
1. B
2. C
3. D
4. B
5. A
6. D
7. B
8. A
9. C
10. B

Pages 12–13
1. B
2. D
3. A
4. C
5. A
6. D
7. C
8. B

Pages 14–15
1. B
2. B
3. C
4. A
5. C
6. D
7. D
8. B
9. A
10. A

Pages 16–17
1. C
2. A
3. B
4. B
5. A
6. C

Pages 18–19
1. B
2. C
3. D
4. A
5. C
6. D
7. C
8. A

9. B
10. D

Pages 20–21
1. B
2. A
3. C
4. B
5. D
6. A
7. D
8. B
9. A
10. C

Pages 22–23
1. B
2. B
3. D
4. B
5. C
6. D

Pages 24–25
1. D
2. C
3. A
4. A
5. B
6. C
7. D
8. A
9. B
10. C
11. A
12. B
13. C
14. A
15. D
16. D
17. B
18. C
19. A
20. B

Pages 26–27
1. A
2. C
3. B
4. D
5. B
6. B
7. C
8. D
9. A
10. C
11. B
12. D

Pages 28–29
1. C
2. D
3. B

4. C
5. D
6. B
7. A
8. B
9. C
10. B

Pages 30–31
1. D
2. C
3. A
4. B
5. B
6. D
7. A
8. C
9. B
10. B
11. A
12. D

Pages 32–33
1. C
2. B
3. A
4. D
5. A
6. B
7. A
8. C
9. A
10. D

Pages 34–35
1. A
2. C
3. B
4. B
5. A
6. D
7. B
8. C
9. D
10. D

Pages 36–37
1. C
2. D
3. B
4. A
5. A
6. C
7. D
8. A
9. C
10. B

Pages 38–39
1. B
2. C
3. A
4. D

5. B
6. C
7. D
8. A
9. B
10. C
11. A
12. C
13. A
14. C
15. D
16. B
17. A
18. A

Pages 40–41
1. B
2. C
3. A
4. A
5. B
6. D
7. C
8. C
9. B
10. A
11. D
12. C
13. B
14. A
15. D
16. B
17. C
18. B
19. A
20. C

Pages 42–43
1. B
2. B
3. D
4. A
5. D
6. A
7. B
8. B
9. A
10. B
11. D
12. B
13. A
14. A
15. A
16. D
17. C
18. D
19. A
20. C

Pages 44–45
1. A
2. C
3. D

4. B
5. A
6. D
7. B
8. B
9. C
10. D
11. B
12. D
13. D
14. A
15. D
16. B
17. C
18. D
19. B
20. D
21. C
22. A

Pages 46–49
1. B
2. A
3. C
4. D
5. D
6. A
7. C
8. B
9. C
10. B
11. A
12. C
13. D
14. A
15. D
16. B
17. C
18. A
19. D
20. B

Page 50
1. B
2. D
3. C
4. D
5. A
6. D
7. C
8. B
9. A

Page 51
1. A
2. B
3. C
4. B
5. B
6. C
7. C
8. C
9. B
10. B
11. B
12. C

Pages 52–53
1. B
2. C
3. C

4. A
5. B
6. C
7. B
8. A
9. D
10. A
11. B
12. C
13. D
14. B
15. A
16. C
17. D
18. A
19. C
20. B
21. D
22. A
23. A
24. B

Pages 54–55
1. A
2. C
3. B
4. D
5. A
6. D
7. A
8. C
9. B
10. D
11. B
12. C
13. B
14. C
15. B
16. A
17. D
18. C
19. D
20. A
21. D
22. A

Page 56
1. A
2. C
3. B
4. A
5. B
6. D
7. B
8. A
9. B
10. C
11. C
12. D

Page 57
1. C
2. A
3. B
4. C
5. A
6. D
7. B
8. D
9. C
10. A

11. B
12. C

Page 58
1. C
2. A
3. B
4. D
5. A
6. D
7. B
8. C
9. D
10. C
11. A
12. B

Page 59
1. C
2. A
3. B
4. C
5. B
6. A
7. A
8. C
9. D
10. D
11. B
12. A

Page 60
1. A
2. B
3. D
4. C
5. B
6. A
7. C
8. D
9. A
10. B
11. C
12. A

Page 61
1. A
2. B
3. C
4. B
5. A
6. D
7. C
8. B
9. A
10. C
11. D
12. D

Pages 62–63
1. C
2. D
3. B
4. B
5. A
6. D
7. A
8. C
9. A
10. B
11. C

12. A
13. B
14. B
15. C
16. B
17. C
18. A
19. B
20. C
21. D

Page 64
1. D
2. A
3. B
4. A
5. B
6. C
7. D
8. D
9. C
10. C

Page 65
1. B
2. A
3. C
4. C
5. C
6. B
7. C
8. B
9. D
10. D

Page 66
1. B
2. A
3. B
4. D
5. B
6. D
7. A
8. C
9. D
10. A
11. B
12. A

Page 67
1. C
2. D
3. C
4. A
5. B
6. A
7. C
8. D
9. A
10. B
11. C
12. A

Page 68
1. A
2. B
3. D
4. B
5. C
6. A
7. C

8. B
9. D
10. D
11. A
12. A

Page 69
1. B
2. A
3. D
4. B
5. A
6. C
7. D
8. B
9. A
10. B
11. D
12. C
13. C
14. B

Page 70
1. C
2. A
3. B
4. D
5. B
6. C
7. B
8. C
9. C
10. D
11. A
12. B
13. C
14. B

Page 71
1. C
2. A
3. B
4. D
5. C
6. B
7. B
8. A
9. D
10. B
11. C
12. D

Page 72
1. B
2. D
3. C
4. A
5. C
6. B
7. D
8. A

Page 73
1. A
2. D
3. B
4. C
5. D
6. A
7. C

8. B

Page 74
1. A
2. C
3. D
4. B
5. C
6. A
7. D
8. A

Page 75
1. B
2. A
3. C
4. A
5. B
6. C
7. B
8. B
9. B
10. D

Page 76
1. B
2. C
3. D
4. C
5. C
6. B
7. C
8. B
9. A

Page 77
1. D
2. C
3. B
4. A
5. B
6. D
7. C
8. D

Page 78
1. D
2. C
3. A
4. B
5. D
6. A
7. B
8. C

Page 79
1. D
2. C
3. A
4. B
5. B
6. D
7. C
8. A

Pages 80–81
1. A
2. D
3. B
4. D

5. B
6. A
7. D
8. C
9. C
10. C
11. B
12. C
13. A
14. A
15. C
16. D

Page 82
1. B
2. A
3. C
4. C
5. D
6. C

Page 83
1. A
2. B
3. C
4. B
5. A
6. C
7. D
8. B

Page 84
1. B
2. A
3. D
4. C
5. D
6. A
7. B
8. C
9. D
10. C
11. A
12. B

Page 85
1. D
2. C
3. A
4. B
5. D
6. B
7. D
8. C

Pages 86–87
1. C
2. A
3. D
4. B
5. A
6. D
7. B
8. C
9. D
10. C
11. D
12. B
13. C
14. A

Pages 88–89
1. B
2. A
3. C
4. C
5. B
6. D
7. C
8. B
9. A
10. B
11. C
12. A
13. D
14. D

Pages 90–93
1. B
2. D
3. A
4. C
5. A
6. C
7. B
8. D
9. C
10. B
11. D
12. A
13. D
14. C
15. A
16. B
17. A
18. D
19. B
20. C
21. A
22. B
23. B
24. D
25. C
26. B
27. B
28. A
29. C
30. B
31. B
32. A
33. C
34. A
35. D
36. C
37. A
38. B
39. B
40. D